MENZIES IN HIS OWN WORDS

A collection of quotes

Edited by David Furse-Roberts

Jeparit Press

Published in 2020 by Connor Court Publishing Pty Ltd under the Jeparit Press Imprint

Jeparit Press is an imprint of Connor Court Publishing in conjunction with the Menzies Research Centre.

Menzies Research Centre
R.G. Menzies House
1 Macquarie St
Barton
ACT 2600
www.menziesrc.org

Connor Court Publishing Pty Ltd
PO Box 7257
Redland Bay QLD 4165
sales@connorcourt.com
www.connorcourt.com
Phone 0497-900-685

Printed in Australia

ISBN: 9781922449351

Front cover design: Vanessa Schimizzi

Dedicated to Heather Henderson AM

Table of Contents

Foreword

It is clear that David Furse-Roberts has done a prodigious amount of work: researching, thinking, writing. It is hard to believe that he never met my father, or heard him speak. I wish he had.

This book gives the reader a very good understanding of what Menzies was like, and what he thought. What it can't do is make it possible to hear him, and feel the atmosphere when he spoke.

Menzies had the ability to get and keep the attention of his audiences. He looked at them, spoke directly to them, somehow created a connection. He also knew how and when to make a light-hearted remark which reinforced the contact. Where did this skill come from?

My father's parents were determined that their children should be well educated and articulate. They would all sit around and take it in turns to read out loud. Their father could not tolerate any mistakes, so they were firmly corrected.

When he was a schoolboy in Ballarat someone gave him a ticket to the South Street Competitions, an annual event for the performing arts. He went, and sat in the middle of a row where he was hemmed in by very large ladies. He could see no way to escape. So he sat through 27 versions of "Friends, Romans, Countrymen", which taught him a lot about how NOT to speak in public.

Those are the only specific things I can recall about how he learnt to speak in public, but the fact is he had strong thespian instincts. After he was made a Knight of the Thistle, Jim Cope called out in Parliament: "You should have got an Oscar, not a Thistle!" Jim was not a mile out.

So, Menzies knew how to get the attention of his audience, but how did he know, so well, what to say?

In Ballarat, still in Primary School, he and his sister lived with their Scottish grandmother. Her form of punishment was to make them learn great slabs of the Bible. That was augmented by his love of poetry and the Classics. Later he won the Shakespeare Society prize, which involved learning hundreds of lines of the prescribed play.

So there he was with a love of words and the English language, and a retentive brain. Those essentials were there. Then he could concentrate on the message he wanted to get across.

In his own words: "When I had a big speech to make in the House, I would begin by making brief notes merely as a reminder to me as to what my line of argument was to be and relying upon the moment to produce the words in which I would clothe the ideas. The night before the speech I read poetry because great poetry gives one a sense of the weight and quality of words which perhaps no other reading can do."

Reading this book, I am constantly surprised and impressed that David Furse-Roberts has the skill and tenacity to find so many appropriate quotes from Menzies. It seems to me he has a magic wand somewhere. We are much in his debt.

- Heather Henderson AM, September 2020

1

A Great and Powerful Friend: Menzies on the American Alliance

Even before the United States entered the Second World War to fight alongside Australian forces in both Europe and the Pacific, Robert Menzies appreciated the bonds of kinship between Australia and the United States. In his own lifetime, Prime Minister Alfred Deakin had invited the American Great White Fleet to visit Australian shores in 1908 and Australian soldiers had fought together with US troops on the Western Front in the Great War. Menzies regarded the history and development of the two countries as analogous with British pioneers crossing vast oceans to explore new continents, build new settlements and forge new democratic civilisations comprised of immigrants drawn from Britain and all of Europe. Australians and Americans therefore both saw the thirst for freedom, the spirit of adventure, the appetite for enterprise, a sturdy self-reliance and a sunny optimism for the future as critical to their common national psyche. At the same time, however, Menzies understood some of the key differences between the two countries, particularly in their system of government and tradition of jurisprudence. Unlike Australia's parliament, the Congress of the United States did not operate according to the British principle of responsible government and Australia's Constitution, in contrast to that of the United States, did not incorporate a Bill of Rights.

The natural affinity of Menzies for the United States became even more apparent following the entry of the United States into the Pacific War with his wartime broadcasts affirming the comradeship between Australian and American forces. Like his Labor opponent, John Curtin, Menzies recognised that Australia needed to defer more to the support of the United States in its campaign to win the war. With the war effort depleting so much of Britain's manpower and resources, the US superseded the UK as the leader of the free world after 1945. While Menzies regarded the historic kinship between Australia and Britain as intimate and imperishable, he appreciated that the Australia of the future would increasingly take its lead from America on security and defence issues. After returning to the prime ministership in 1949, he visited New York in 1950 to give assurance to Australia's decision to commit troops to the Korean War. This was followed by an address to the US Congress in Washington, where he expressed Australia's solidarity with America in the defence of freedom and democracy. On his 1950 visit to the United States, Menzies was invested as a Chief Commander of the Legion of Merit.

In a measure to formalise the US-Australian alliance, the Menzies government signed the ANZUS Treaty in San Francisco on 1 September 1951, a foreign policy decision that Menzies would recall with pride as one of the greatest achievements of his government. The architects of the historic Treaty were Menzies' Minister for External Affairs, Percy Spender, and the US Secretary of State in the Truman Administration, Dean Acheson. The mutual security pact bound Australia, New Zealand and the United States to recognise that an armed attack in the Pacific area on any of the parties would endanger the peace and safety of the others. Despite Britain agitating to join ANZUS in the early 1950s, the Treaty remained confined to a partnership between the three Pacific nations. In addition to codifying Australian-American defence and security ties through ANZUS, the Menzies government cemented the alliance through a second pact, the South East Asia Treaty Organisation (SEATO). Executed in Manilla on 18 November 1954, the Treaty sought to engage the United States, Australia and New Zealand in the security and defence of South East Asia. Unlike the ANZUS pact, it included the United Kingdom and France, together with several other Asia Pacific nations including Pakistan, Thailand and the Philippines. SEATO was formed as a direct response to Western fears of communist expansion in South East Asia following the retreat of the French from Vietnam after their defeat in the battle of Dien Bien Phu in April 1954.

Through the ANZUS and SEATO treaties, Australia and the United States forged closer defense and security ties during Menzies' post-war Prime Ministership. The first major conflict since the 1950-53 Korean War in which Australian troops fought alongside American forces was of course the Vietnam War. As John Howard pointed out, it was actually Menzies himself, and not his successor Harold Holt, who decided in 1964 that Australia would join the United States in the military campaign in South Vietnam. Menzies thus emerged as not only a sympathiser of the American venture in South Vietnam but an active participant. He concurred with the American perspective that the conflict in Vietnam represented a clash of civilisations between authoritarian regimes beholden to materialistic communism and free countries steeped in religious faith. For Menzies, it was the common defence of free and democratic ideals in the Asia Pacific that brought Australia and the United States ever closer together.

In recognition of his close affinity with the United States, Robert Menzies was appointed Scholar-in-Residence at the University of Virginia shortly after his retirement as Prime Minister in 1966. Returning to the University where he had delivered his Thomas Jefferson Oration in July 1963, Menzies gave a series of lectures later published as *Central Power in the Australian Commonwealth* (1967). For Menzies, the US-Australian alliance embodied a mixture of pragmatism and idealism. At one level, it was based upon a mutual interest to maintain defence and security in the Asia Pacific, but in a deeper sense, it was rooted in a common resolve by the two English-speaking democracies to advance the ideals of human freedom as the great antidote to tyranny and oppression.

"Not only do we [Americans and Australians] speak the same language, but to a large extent we have the same thoughts and we act in the same way. We are both equally devoted to the rights of man. We are both unhesitatingly and resolutely opposed to the overthrowing of those rights by any tyrant. Both of us...have had a similar history, a history in which industrial skill and power and rising standards of living have followed upon a pioneer age in which foundations were built by brave and adventurous people who knew how to dare the unknown and greet the unseen with a cheer"

Robert Menzies, Broadcast to the People of the United States of America, 4 July 1941

"You and we may live in vast countries, separated by thousands of miles of sea, but on the matters that count in this world we stand on common ground. On these matters we are united by the Pacific and not separated by it. We Australians have entered, like you, into the rich inheritance bequeathed by Washington and Hamilton, and Jefferson, and John Marshall, and Abraham Lincoln."

Robert Menzies, Broadcast to the People of the United States of America, 4 July 1941

"Many millions of United States citizens have their family origin in Germany, Italy, Russia, Poland, [and] the Scandinavian countries. We cannot automatically think of the United States any longer as an Anglo-Saxon community, but we can and do think of it with great pride and satisfaction as a community in which the language, the literature, the institutions and the ideals of the British people have taken root and flowered"

Robert Menzies, Our American Allies, Broadcast, 23 January 1942

"The fortunes and aspirations of Australia are linked with those of Great Britain 'for better or for worse; for richer or poorer; till death do us part' – but it is a great thing for us to have such allies as these Americans. We are together now for the urgent saving of the world"

Robert Menzies, Our American Allies, Broadcast, 23 January 1942

"The truth is that when we Australians think about the other people of the world we think of some of them as foreigners and some of them as not. I want to tell you at once that except in the jaundiced eye of the law, Americans are not foreigners in Australia"

Robert Menzies, Address to the United States Congress, Washington, 1 August 1950

"If we recall that these elements in our common history have an enormous background of common inheritance of a history before the late 18th Century, of language and literature, of the Common Law of the great principles enshrined in the phrase 'the rule of law', of popular self-government, of religious faith, and of a common passion for individual and national freedom, we will at once see that enmity between the United States and Australia would be not only unthinkable, but 'most foul, strange, and unnatural'"

Robert Menzies, 'American – Australian Relations: What are they and Why?', Riecker Memorial Lecture Number 12, University of Arizona, 1967

"It is not to be wondered, or scoffed at, that we have a friendship with you, for we know that you have the same principles. Our unwritten alliance with the United States is a spiritual one"

Robert Menzies, 'American – Australian Relations: What are they and Why?', Riecker Memorial Lecture Number 12, University of Arizona, 1967

"Of course, we have great things in common; our language; much of our literature; democratic self-government; the rule of law; the 'Common Law' itself: Australia and the United States are both within the inheritance of the English Common Law. We have similar ideas, and indeed instincts, about the relation of the State to the individual, and this provides us with the basis of our notions of freedom. Add to this, in the case of Australia, a Federal Constitution in some important ways modelled upon your own, a vivid and imperishable association in two great wars, and the total represents an amazing community of thought and tradition"

Robert Menzies, The American machinery of government compared with that of Australia, 1968

"We in Australia, of course, are British, if I may say so, to the boot heels. But we also happen to be people who have for the United States and for the people of the United States a tremendous feeling, not just of friendship or respect, but of affection"

Robert Menzies, "Anglo-American Friendship", Address to members of the American-Australian Association, New York, 20 May 1953

"We are ever mindful of the warmth of relations between ourselves and the people, of the United States of America – an association which I am sure can only grow in strength as both our countries work together in the cause of freedom and justice within the framework of the democratic way of life"

Robert Menzies, Message to Governor of the State of Arizona, 29 August 1962

"Australia has a deep feeling for your country, not just because your friendship contributes so greatly to our national security, but basically because, great or small, we work for the same kind of free world"

Robert Menzies, Jefferson Oration, The Battle for Freedom, Charlottesville, Virginia, 4 July 1963

"What is present with us is that we have a relationship with the United States which is not the relationship between a benefactor and a pensioner. It is, I am happy to say, a proud relationship between friends"

Robert Menzies, White House Luncheon, Washington, 24 June 1964

2

Australian National Identity

Famously remembered for his aphorism that he was 'British to the boot-heels', Menzies proudly declared in public that he was also 'an Australian through and through'. Whilst Menzies saw himself as British in the sense that he was devoted to cultivating British traditions such as the English Common Law, Parliamentary Democracy, the Constitutional Monarchy and the English language, he saw himself as unequivocally Australian in his post-war resolve to develop the island continent into a resourceful, confident nation with a cohesive society and robust economy. Even as wartime Prime Minister from 1939-1941, Menzies' loyalty to Australia had been manifest when he attempted to make a forthright case for the nation's defence interests in South East Asia before a somewhat obstinate British Prime Minister in 1941, with Churchill then only having a limited understanding of the Pacific theatre. Never forgetting his origins as a 'scholarship boy' from rural Victoria, Menzies saw his personal past, present and future as intertwined with that of Australia. As such, he maintained an abiding interest in reinforcing Australia's national identity as the country modernised economically and socially after WWII.

Conscious that Australia was still a relatively young nation, Menzies saw post-war Australia as 'still on the threshold of our national life'. For Menzies, one of the great impulses behind the historical formation of Australia's national character was the 'pioneering spirit'. From the Governor of NSW, Lachlan Macquarie, to the convict-turned-architect, Francis Greenway, many of Australia's early convicts, settlers, explorers and gold prospectors of the colonial age were doughty pioneers of initiative, enterprise and resourcefulness. Overcoming all manner of geographical and social obstacles, they had toiled under foreign skies to cultivate the land, build roads, schools and hospitals, establish businesses and institute new parliaments and courts. Drawing on inherited British customs and traditions to forge a free and progressive civilisation in the antipodes, Australia's pioneers epitomised the values that Menzies so admired. The Australian pioneering spirit, however, was not simply a historical phenomenon to be celebrated in the bush ballads and folklore of old, but an enduring ethos that was sorely needed in the present to drive the nation forward to future greatness. Menzies warned that if Australians do not live as 'pioneers' *today*, the future vitality and prosperity of the nation would be at stake.

Repudiating the insular conception of Australian national identity that had held sway in the early years of Federation, Menzies welcomed postwar immigration as an opportunity for Australia to cement its own sense of itself. Appreciating that Australia had always been a nation of immigrants; Menzies regarded the new wave of European arrivals in the 1950s and 60s as the great heirs to the colonial free settlers from Britain and Ireland who had contributed so much to the development of the country in the past century. Like the previous generations of free settlers, the post-war immigrants were seen by Menzies as present-day exemplars of the pioneering spirit that had built Australia. In their boldness of spirit to uproot from the 'old world' of Europe to start afresh in a new homeland, they exhibited the thirst for discovery, adventure, enterprise and achievement which would only give new breath to Australia's pioneering spirit. With post-war immigrants opening new businesses in Australia's cities and contributing to national public works programmes such as the Snowy Mountains Hydro-electric Scheme, they would tread in the footsteps of those earlier arrivals who had mined the earth and laid the first roads and railways. Thus through a sustained programme of post-war immigration, Australia's national identity would be fortified and not eroded.

While Menzies was an impenitent believer in the British tenets of Australia's civilisation and culture, he did not hold these to be race-specific.

Despite continuing restrictions on non-European immigration to Australia, an individual no longer needed to be of Anglo-Saxon extraction to be deemed free to participate in national life as a full Australian citizen. Indeed, Menzies went so far as to envisage a future time when the nation would be led by a prime minister with a non-Anglo-Saxon name. Essentially, his faith in the genius of British traditions, such as the English language and the English Common Law, to be received into the diverse ethnic groups of the Commonwealth gave him assurance that an increasingly multi-racial Australia could pose no challenge to their perpetuity. Thus in contrast to earlier Australian nationalists such as James Edmond of *The Bulletin* and Prime Minister Billy Hughes, Menzies did not see Australia's cultural identity as necessarily contingent on the preservation of a homogenous, Anglo-Saxon population.

In common, however, with older forms of Australian patriotism, Menzies had an evident affection for the Australian bush as the wellspring of national virtues and ideals. In the tradition of Banjo Paterson and the bush poets, he spoke warmly of Australian country life as fostering the ideals of a 'sturdy individualism' and a 'rugged patriotism'. In the face of adversity, the outback explorer, the small-town entrepreneur, the miner and the farmer on the land were esteemed for embodying the pioneering spirit of resourcefulness and dogged resilience. The contribution of rural folklore to Australia's national identity was not lost on Menzies when he lauded Waltzing Matilda as 'superbly Australian'. As Prime Minister, Menzies understood the importance of the 'bush' to Australian life and sought to advance the interests of the rural community by working in close concert with the Country Party.

As well as cherishing the old pioneering virtues, Menzies' sense of Australian national identity also appealed to newer expressions of nationhood, particularly the notion of Australia as a *whole*. Although this had been championed earlier by Sir Henry Parkes and the other pioneers of Australian Federation, it was reinforced by Menzies and given concrete form in the consolidation of Canberra as the national capital. Despite remaining a federalist, Menzies was anxious to overcome the handicap of state parochialism to emphasise that citizens were Australians first before they were Tasmanians or Queenslanders. To provide all Australians with a tangible focal point of national identity and a national capital in which they could all take immense pride, Menzies committed his government to developing Canberra.   In 1957, the government established the National Capital Development Commission as an independent statutory authority charged with overseeing the planning and development of the city. During Menzies' time in office, the great bulk of the federal public service moved from the state capitals to Canberra and Lake Burley Griffin was inaugurated in October 1964. The new city emerging around the glimmering shores of Lake Burley Griffin represented not only the crown of the Australian Commonwealth, but a uniquely Australian creation with its founding suburbs, streets, parks and buildings bearing the names of Australian leaders and pioneers.

"In spite of some of the present buildings, Canberra may well become the Athens of Australia; if it does it will be the result not of works of stone or bronze but of the twin spirits of learning and responsibility"

Robert Menzies, The Place of a University in a Modern Community, 1939

"A nation is like a river. It will rise no higher than its source."

Robert Menzies, The Individual in the New Order, City Hall, Brisbane, 21 January 1943

"There cannot be a prosperous Australia with a bankrupt countryside; there can be no healthy balance in our social and political structure if there is a depopulated countryside; there can be no adequate contribution by Australia to a revival of world trade and a restoration of living standards unless strong primary industries are able to export their products competitively to the world's markets"

Robert Menzies, Rural Policy, Broadcast, 9 July 1943

"Country life has things to offer to the intelligent mind that no city can surpass. It breeds sanity and balance and philosophy. It offers health and strength, a sturdy individualism and a rugged patriotism which has been a strong foundation for us in two wars"

Robert Menzies, Rural Policy, Broadcast, 9 July 1943

"First, we are Australians; not remote and scattered colonists but a closely-knit nation, building our traditions for the future upon the noble traditions of the past; adding to them, as we trust, the products of our own character, conflicts and achievements"

Robert Menzies, Broadcast on the Occasion of Australia's Jubilee Celebrations, 9 May 1951

"It is my honour to speak for a peaceful and friendly nation, not given to bitter enmities, nor to sustained hatreds; a nation living in a land of sunshine and cheerfulness and goodwill"

Robert Menzies, Broadcast on the Occasion of Australia's Jubilee Celebrations, 9 May 1951

"I am a dyed-in-the-wool Australian, and I believe in Australia. I think that we are a good country and a good people."

Robert Menzies, 'Australia Today – Man to Man', Broadcast, 26 August 1953

"The people who came out to Australia in the fifties and sixties of the last century, were not the weaklings of the old world. They were on the contrary, people who had enough boldness and vigour of spirit to pull up their roots in an old world and take their chances in a new."

Robert Menzies, 'Australia Today – Man to Man', Broadcast, 2 September 1953

"The Australian farmer is living a most useful life. He has, if he chooses, a good life, with some time for reflection, living close to nature, getting and applying the benefit of scientific research and contributing most powerfully to the over-all wellbeing of every person in Australia"

Robert Menzies, 'Australia Today – Man to Man', Broadcast, 14 October 1953

"If there are great developments in this young country in the next few years, it will be because there are pioneers now, thinking, and planning, and having visions for the future. When we give up being pioneers, and rest on our national laurels, and live on the fruit of the efforts of the past, development will cease, national life will become selfish and stagnant, and our standards of living will steadily fall"

Robert Menzies, 'Australia Today – Man to Man', Broadcast, 7 April 1954

"We have a rapidly growing population, a great and potentially rich inheritance, and increasing significance and responsibility in world affairs. In the course of a century Australia may well be one of the very great factors in the peace and progress of mankind"

Robert Menzies, 'Australia Today – Man to Man', Broadcast, 7 April 1954

"We are the pioneers of what can and must become a great and powerful and wise and generous nation. This is not an expression of self-satisfaction, but of proper humility and sense of world duty"

Robert Menzies, 'Australia Today – Man to Man', Broadcast, 7 April 1954

"We need workers with hand, heart and head, if we are to become a great nation"

Robert Menzies, Election Speech, 5 May 1954

"No nation does well to forget its past; but no nation can live on its past. It is on what we do now and in the future that somebody else's history will someday depend"

Robert Menzies, Australia Day, Broadcast, 26 January 1955

"Waltzing Matilda…is unquestionably Australia's national song, with a nice lilt in it"

Robert Menzies, Speeches in Honour of R G Menzies, 5 March 1955

"If you go around Australia and look at what has been done and what is being done, you constantly remind yourselves that this was done by the ancient pioneering virtues that made Australia, work done by simple people who worked in their day and generation, who

were as honest as the day…God-fearing people who believed in their families and in their future and in their country"

Robert Menzies, Speech at Finney's Auditorium Brisbane, 22 July 1955

"There has been a sort of conflict between what are thought to be the interests of the primary producers and the interests of the secondary industries. My own private belief is that each needs the other in Australia"

Robert Menzies, Opening of the Heinz Company, Dandenong, 10 October 1955

"We have a small but rapidly growing population inhabiting a great island continent. We are aware of our responsibilities. We still believe that the spirit of our pioneers is not dead. But there can be no doubt in these days that the growth of any nation can be vastly and rapidly stimulated by the friendly sentiment and practical interest of other people"

Robert Menzies, Opening of Congress of the International Olympic Committee, Melbourne, 19 November, 1956

"We in Australia pride ourselves on having a feeling of adventure and courage, and if I may so to you, we are far better known around the world for those two qualities than we are for anything else and let us keep it so"

R. G. Menzies, Liberal Party Rally, Cottesloe (WA), 8 March 1958

A sense of community, a sense of common destiny, a firm conviction that our own free efforts will advance the country, a feeling of liberty, a feeling that we're not going to be dragooned and regimented into ways of life which we don't approve of, a feeling of free pride. Give us all these things, as we have them now, and I venture to say that in this very place, in a hundred years' time, somebody at present unknown who may have a name not at all Anglo-Saxon…may be standing here as the Prime Minister talking to you with pride about a free, enlightened country of fifty millions of people able to give service to mankind in a new century and of an order that the world will not forget.

R. G. Menzies, Liberal Party Rally, Cottesloe (WA), 8 March 1958

"We'll have to develop more and more a sense of community. We're not West Australians first you know, or Victorians first, we're Australian.

R. G. Menzies, Liberal Party Rally, Cottesloe (WA), 8 March 1958

"National pride is deeply founded on a sense of history, of self-respect, of achievement. The nations which have contributed most to the history of the improvement of mankind have been those in which a sense of national unity was predominant"

Robert Menzies, 'Australia Today – Man to Man', 23 April 1958

"The strength of the community depends upon its internal friendliness and its spirit of cooperation and mutual understanding so that industries, primary and secondary, learn that they are dependent on each other and employers and employees learn that they are dependent on each other"

Robert Menzies, Snowy Mountains Scheme, 13 September 1958

"In a period in which we in Australia are still, I think, handicapped by parochialism, by a slight distrust of big ideas or of big people or of big enterprises, a slight nervousness about them all. In an age of this kind, this scheme is teaching us and everybody in Australia to think in a big way to be thankful for big things to be proud of big enterprises…and to be thankful for big men"

Robert Menzies, Snowy Mountains Scheme, 13 September 1958

"What Australians want is good and honest government, with administrators who pursue steadfast policies, encourage growth, foster individual enterprise, preserve freedom, and maintain Australia's place in the world"

Robert Menzies, Election Speech, 29 October 1958

"We are determined to help to bring about, in our land, a rapidly growing population of free people, rising production and social wealth, increasing skill and intellectual competence, with emphasis upon the individual and his dignity and independence and, through these priceless elements, the emergence of an Australia

powerful and responsible, adequately furnished in material terms but even more richly furnished with those mental and spiritual qualities which have made our race great in the past and will make it greater in the future"

Robert Menzies, Election Speech, 29 October 1958

"One of these days...I will sit down and try to write some words of somewhat more or somewhat less criminal quality, because Waltzing Matilda to me is a great air and wherever I have heard it in the world, it brings me right back home"

Robert Menzies, 71st Annual Association Day Banquet at the Commercial Travellers' Association of NSW, 13 August 1960

"The security of Australia is not only dear to us who are grown up, it is even more dear to our children and our grandchildren and the whole future of a nation, which I am quite determined in my own mind, is destined to be one of the great and proud, and free, and responsible, and contributing nations of the world"

Robert Menzies, 71st Annual Association Day Banquet at the Commercial Travellers' Association of NSW, 13 August 1960

"In the course of my own lifetime, Australia has moved from being a predominantly agricultural and pastoral country to being a very great industrial power. And that is, of course, a great revolution, a great and beneficial one"

Robert Menzies, Speech at the Opening of Warner-Lambert Pty Ltd, Sydney, 9 September 1960.

"I like to believe, and I think I am right in believing that Australia has a significance in the world of affairs rather more than the population of our country would warrant. We are regarded, increasingly, as a notable country, as a happy country as a country with an immense future, and as a country made up of people who have good common sense and courage"

Robert Menzies, Citizens Luncheon, Ashfield Town Hall, 15 May 1961

"The real point is that we are an adult country, far more adult, far wiser in judgment, though I say it myself, than some countries with many times our population. And we must have in relation to these matters, a decent pride for this is a remarkably great country"

Robert Menzies, Citizens Luncheon, Ashfield Town Hall, 15 May 1961

"The great thing is to have a belief in the people of Australia, which I have profoundly deep down in me, a belief that this is a nation of honest, decent people who respect firmness, who respect what they believe to be intelligence, and who are honest and are not looking for some cheap advantage. We must have faith in ourselves because we have faith in our people."

Robert Menzies, Liberal Party Rally, Brisbane City Hall, 21 June 1961

"We are a friendly people. We are not stuffy. We are not consumed by snobberies of class, or some of this nonsense that has beset some of the older countries of the world. You are in an essentially democratic country where every man has a chance to stand on his own feet, and every woman, and to be taken at his or her own true value by other people. Nothing could be better than that: to be free, to feel that there is no shadow over you, to feel that there is none of the paraphernalia of dictatorship in this country, that we are, in the truest sense, a friendly community, a brotherhood, and a sisterhood of people"

Robert Menzies, Naturalisation Ceremony, Perth, 24 July 1961

"We want a progressive nation. There is nothing for the young in this country that can attract them or us, unless it is the vision of progress for the future, but above all things, we want a civilised nation. Not a nation in which every political issue is determined in terms of pounds, shillings and pence. Not a materialistic nation, but a nation that tunes itself to high endeavour and to great ideals, a civilised nation."

Robert Menzies, Young Liberals Rally, Hawthorn, 6 July 1962

"We could easily become man for man, woman for woman, the richest country in the Southern Hemisphere, but it won't matter very

much unless we can say that we are the most civilised country in the Southern Hemisphere. Civilised because we understand the unselfish duties of citizenship; civilised because we have come to understand the importance of the human being, the dignity of the human being, the dignity of labour, the responsibility of riches. These are the tests of civilisation, and our great task is to produce a civilised nation"

Robert Menzies, WA Convention of the Liberal Party, South Perth Civic Centre, 30 July 1962

"This island continent came out of the mists; it was developed by people who had the spirit of adventure... And without that spirit of adventure, Australia can't become by the turn of the century the great and powerful and respected country to whose noises I would hope to listen from the grave"

Robert Menzies, WA Convention of the Liberal Party, South Perth Civic Centre, 30 July 1962

"Australia Day is an occasion for renewing our determination to build soundly on the existing foundations, to develop new resources, to build up a wider and fuller civilisation. In short, we must see ourselves as the present pioneers of an even better Australian future"

Robert Menzies, Australia Day Message, Canberra, 25 January 1963

"It is in the Australian character not to prolong hatreds, or to live on past events. We are essentially a forward-looking people, with a great instinct for optimism and friendship. We want to live not only in peace, but in the widest cooperation with other nations"

Robert Menzies, Luncheon in Honour of Japan PM, Canberra, 30 September 1963

"We are all members one of another. This is something we must never lose sight of, and whether we be Catholic or Protestant or Jewish or Muslim, the end remains clear: We have an overwhelming duty to serve our country on the highest level and to the best of our talents"

Robert Menzies, The Cardinal's Dinner, Sydney, 30 July 1964

"In my opinion Alfred Deakin was the greatest Prime Minister this

country ever had and if we ever have one as good in the future, we will be doing very well...All the foundational policies, not only in the fiscal field, in the defence field, in the industrial field, the pattern of national policy which we have come to accept so much in Australia was laid down by this remarkable man"

Robert Menzies, Handing over the Papers of Alfred Deakin to the National Library of Australia, 3 December, 1965

"I am delighted to think that after all these years I can look around my country and say, this is a strong country; its people are prospering, its population has grown; it does matter in the world and is listened to with respect in the world"

Robert Menzies, Press, Radio and Television Conference, Canberra, 20 January 1966

"Now Waltzing Matilda is superbly Australian. In other words it's immoral, it's all about a sheep stealer but it's musical. It has much in common with some Australians you know"

Robert Menzies, Speech at Dover's Maison Dieu (Town Hall), 20 July 1966

"At best we still have the pioneering spirit. The early pioneers are buried in many old cemeteries; but their descendants are not degenerate. They may look different from their predecessors seen in old and faded photographs or engravings; but they have the spirit of discovery in new fields of endeavour and enterprise"

Robert Menzies, 'American – Australian Relations: What are they and Why?', Riecker Memorial Lecture Number 12, University of Arizona, 1967

"I was sustained in my political life for over 20 years by one firm belief and that was that the vast majority of the Australian people are good and decent people"

Robert Menzies, Conferral of the Freedom of the City of Kew, 11 August 1974

3

Britain and the Commonwealth

Throughout his life, Menzies made no secret of his pride in both his own British identity and the British heritage of Australia. In the public consciousness, he is famously remembered for his repeated aphorism that he was 'British to the bootstraps'. As an Anglophile Scot, Menzies idealised what he saw as 'Englishness' in a set of cultural traditions dating back to the earliest days of Magna Carta. These traditions included the English language and the English canon of literature featuring the King James Bible and the works of Shakespeare, the monarchy, the philosophy of English liberalism represented by Gladstone and Asquith, the Westminster parliamentary system with its practice of responsible government, the rule of law, the English common law, and Test cricket. While steeped in British cultural influences from the time of his birth, Menzies did not visit Britain itself until he had reached his forties. On his voyage to Britain in 1935, he spotted the White Cliffs of Dover and wrote in his diary that 'my journey to Mecca is ended'. In that same year, Menzies penned an essay for the *Australian Quarterly* on 'Australia's Place in the Empire' to affirm the kinship between the two countries. According to Menzies, Australia and Britain had to deal with their relationship 'not on mere terms of friendship' but as 'members of the same family'. As Prime Minister from 1939-1941, Menzies responded to Britain's declaration of war on Nazi Germany on 3 September 1939 by declaring that 'Australia was also at war'. In so doing, he expressed Australia's instinctive solidarity with Britain as members of a 'great family of nations' involved in a struggle 'which we must at all costs win'.

In the post-war period, Menzies' pride in Britain manifested itself in his foreign policy decisions to support British interests, his devotion to the British Commonwealth of Nations, his public displays of enthusiasm for Royal visits to Australia, his frequent apologia for the Westminster system of parliamentary democracy and his regular appearances at Test cricket matches. Whilst forging deeper defence and security ties with the United States through the ANZUS and SEATO treaties, Menzies and his government was resolved to retain similarly close ties with Britain. Shortly after returning as Prime Minister in 1949, Menzies supported the British-led campaign in the Malaya Emergency by sending Caribou transport aircraft and Lincoln bombers in July 1950, followed by ground troops in 1955. Menzies again supported British forces in the Indonesian-Malaysian Confrontation when Australia sent a Strategic Reserve battalion to Borneo in rotation with British and Malaysian units. Even with the Suez Crisis of 1956 driving a sharp wedge between Britain and the United States, Menzies supported Britain's efforts to regain control of the Suez Canal from Egypt. He justified his stance on the basis that 'the United Kingdom should retain power, prestige and moral influence' in the interests of adhering to the UN Charter and maintaining world peace. Menzies' hope for Britain's continuing frontline role on the world stage also explained his governments' decision to allow British nuclear testing on Australian territory in the early 1950s. On the domestic front, meanwhile, Menzies passionately defended the parliamentary and legal institutions Australia had inherited from Britain.

In his last year of office, there were two events that underscored Menzies' abiding affection for Britain. The first was the visible part he played in the funeral service for Sir Winston Churchill at London's St Paul's Cathedral on 30 January 1965, where he participated as a pallbearer and eulogist. The second was Menzies' appointment to the ceremonial position as Lord Warden of the Cinque Ports and Constable of Dover Castle. Succeeding

Churchill in this prestigious British post, he became the first non-Briton to occupy it in 900 years. Menzies used the occasion of his installation to remind the assembled audience of dignitaries of the continuity of British history.

Following his retirement in 1966, his zeal for the British connection continued unabated. Where health permitted, he visited Britain on a regular basis and presided over the inauguration of the Australia-Britain Society on 26 August 1971. In his address to the Society, he remarked that a decade or so earlier, such an association would have been deemed unnecessary considering that the links between Australia and Britain were always assumed as a given. As Britain, however, became more economically integrated with Europe, Menzies perceived a need for Australia to renew and cherish its old ties with Britain even as Australia as an 'adult nation' had to pursue its own interests and considerations.

Integral to Menzies' association with Britain was his intimate engagement with the Commonwealth of Nations and its affairs. Born in 1894, Menzies had grown up in a world where school atlases displayed maps sporting great areas of red to symbolise Britain's dominion over an empire on which the 'sun never set'. Right up until the Second World War, the British Empire had represented an unshakable citadel of the civilised world for Menzies and many of his fellow Australians. During his postwar Prime Ministership, however, Menzies witnessed the transformation of this global body from an empire of colonial dependencies to an association of largely independent states, many of which had become Republics by 1966. Whilst the staunchly monarchist Menzies had regretted this development, he had 'learned to live with it', believing that a new Commonwealth of equals still held immense value as an association of countries drawn together by a common British heritage. As in the earlier days of the empire, Commonwealth Prime Ministers could still meet in conferences to discuss views and make pronouncements on shared ideas. In the interests of preserving Commonwealth unanimity, Menzies held strictly to the principle of non-interference in the domestic affairs of member countries. Thus when the issue of South Africa's apartheid regime arose in 1960, Menzies, whilst opposed to apartheid, did not endorse any action by the Commonwealth to censure South Africa over its internal policies for fear of causing a rift within the Commonwealth. For Menzies, the priority of preserving the integrity of the association took precedence over confronting South Africa about its domestic affairs.

"It says a great deal for the basic character of the British people that from the days of the Magna Carta to the giving of votes to women in the Twentieth Century the movement towards democratic freedom has gone on"

Robert Menzies, Freedom and the Call to Action, Lecture to Junior Chamber of Commerce, 4 August 1947

"For tradition, to the Englishman, is not a barren pride in departed glories; it is something from which he derives a profound assurance, a sense of destiny, and a determination never to abandon what has been purchased with such valour and endurance by those who have gone before him"

Robert Menzies, The English Tradition, The New York Times Magazine, 10 July 1949

"I am British, and British to the boot heels and I have an undying affection for the Old Country"

Robert Menzies, Speech at Finney's Auditorium Brisbane, 22 July 1955

"Let me say, quite plainly, that the whole lively and evolving history of the British Empire and the British Commonwealth of Nations was not the product of any theory. It has been from first to last, a practical matter, an inductive process, like the slow creation of the Common Law and of all the great instruments of self-government"

Robert Menzies, Suez Canal, Statement by the Prime Minister, House of Representatives, 25 September 1956

"If Great Britain has not as yet fired a satellite into space, she has, by a creative modern policy converted colonies into independent nations, founded upon parliamentary sovereignty and enriched by the rule of law, while the Soviet Union has been busy converting independent nations into colonies under the rule not of law, but of the tank and the bomb"

Robert Menzies, Address to the Tenth Session of the Australasian Medical Congress, Hobart, 5 March 1958

"We are the inheritors of British liberty. And among its greatest defenders in the world!"

Robert Menzies, Speech at Orange, 24 October 1960

"In the whole of recorded modern history this was, I believe, the one occasion when one man [Winston Churchill], with one soaring imagination, with one fire burning in him, and with one unrivalled capacity for conveying it to others, won a crucial victory not only for the forces (for there were many heroes in those days) but for the very spirit of human freedom"

Robert Menzies, Funeral of Sir Winston Churchill, 30 January 1965

"Never fall into the error of thinking or speaking patronizingly of Britain and her now disappearing Empire. For, though her colonial days are almost over, and new nations, once colonies, have emerged...the best elements and institutions in these new nations have been derived from their former masters. There is a species of immortality about good things. It is our belief in this great truth which gives us courage and persistence"

Robert Menzies, 'American – Australian Relations: What are they and Why?', Riecker Memorial Lecture Number 12, University of Arizona, 1967

"Our roots are deep in history; and that history was for centuries made in the motherland of our race. Parliamentary self-government; the common law; the rule of law; honest administration; the rights of minorities; social justice; the great virtues of loyalty and patriotism, of courage in adversity. The realisation that our common allegiance to the Crown is not a proof of subservience but

of national unity and human dignity"

Robert Menzies, Melbourne Scots – 'Father and Son' Night, 1968

"How could you fail to be an anglophile if you walk around with your eyes open and your ears open and you know that the whole system of law under which you live came to us from Westminster, if you know that the whole system of parliamentary government came to us from Westminster, that responsible government in Australia came to us from Westminster, if you know that the scrupulous and honest administration of the law, the incorruptibility of judges, the high traditions of the civil service came to us from Great Britain"

Robert Menzies, Address at English Speaking Union Dinner, Melbourne, 26 February 1970

"Everything we have in this country as we look around has its British origin. Parliament, a free Press, a popularly elected Government, upright Justice, these things – the rule of Law – these are the matters which are essential to Australian self-government and we would be a lot of damnable fools if we forget 'the pit from which we were hewn' because you refresh your mind and your spirit when you remember usefully and when you remember consciously about what has happened and how it came about"

Robert Menzies, Speech to Australia-Britain Society, Melbourne, 29 April 1971

"We didn't come into existence by some divine intervention. We came into existence because Great Britain was the great colonising power in the world and because the Dutch having missed the opportunity and the French having missed the opportunity, we are of British stock. They brought all that they had to us…What they did bring was the British character, the British guts and determination, the British respect for other people, the British instinct for justice, for self-government on the widest possible basis. These are great things"

Robert Menzies, Speech to Australia-Britain Society, Melbourne, 29 April 1971

"We've become an adult nation – we have our own interests, our own economic interests, our own trade considerations; but that doesn't remove us from the family"

Robert Menzies, Australia-Britain Society Inaugural Dinner, Sydney, 26 August 1971

"The Scots have made a positive contribution all around the world. They don't suffer from the unhappy disease of looking back on their grievances and living on their grievances. On the contrary, they look forward, and the Scots throughout modern history have shown that wherever they go in the world they make a contribution to the country to which they have gone and to the good order and government of that country. The Scots are forward looking, not backward looking, and that is tremendously important"

Robert Menzies, Speech at Melbourne Scots Dinner for St Andrew's Night, 24 November 1973

4

Character, Virtue and Civilisation

Amidst his public pronouncements on routine matters of policy such as fiscal management, foreign affairs, defence, health and education, Menzies found occasions to ruminate on the deeper questions of human character and virtue that he regarded as lying at the heart of Western civilisation and the survival of its free ideals. The human carnage wrought by two world wars and the steady rise of material prosperity in the post-war years were two of the great twentieth-century phenomena that prompted Menzies to focus on matters of the heart and spirit. With his appeals to honesty, self-sacrifice, community service, tolerance and individuality, his basic conception of character represented a synthesis of his Presbyterian faith and liberal philosophy. Like his messages on public speaking and the English language, his exhortations to cultivate moral character were frequently directed to younger audiences at school speech nights and assemblies. Menzies understood that the rising generation of Australians would be responsible for determining the future character of the country he presently led.

Appreciating that the two gruesome world wars of the twentieth-century were not merely geopolitical conflagrations but the product of corrupted human hearts consumed by enmity and malice, Menzies firmly believed that the restoration of good moral character in the souls of men and women was key to rebuilding modern civilisation from the rubble of war and strife. While applauding the tremendous contribution of medicine, science and technology to twentieth-century civilisation, Menzies argued that these advances must never come at the expense of nurturing spiritual and moral values. As the calamitous course of the twentieth-century had testified, it was impossible for modern break-throughs in health and quality of life to usher in a better world without human beings better understanding and valuing one another. The other development that necessitated a focus on the moral and spiritual was the rapid growth of material prosperity in the post-war decades. The Menzies era witnessed steady increases in both home and car ownership amongst Australian families, with the proliferation of new household appliances offering an unprecedented quality of life. Menzies was conscious that the policies of his own government had contributed to this greater affluence and he welcomed it as a sign of national progress. At the same time, nonetheless, he reminded Australians that politics was more than a mere matter of 'loaves and fishes' and that 'man did not live by bread alone'. In whatever age and circumstance, the simple virtues of integrity and service to others would always trump materialistic considerations of wealth and status.

Like the very ideal of freedom itself, Menzies held that moral character was primarily cultivated within the heart and mind of the individual. Character sprang from the combination of an individual's personal beliefs and life experiences which were moulded by one's family upbringing, education, religious instruction and peer relations. For this reason, governments could not be expected to cultivate moral virtues in their citizens simply by passing new laws or creating new departments. When speaking at charity events, Menzies would remind his audience that there could be no 'Department of Loving Kindness' or 'Minister for Loving Kindness'. Loving acts of kindness to others flowed from the heart and mind of the individual and were not deeds that people could mechanically outsource to their governments to perform. While governments had an important role to play in passing laws and criminal codes to restrain human wickedness, Menzies saw families, schools, churches and voluntary associations as the great incubators of personal character. Indeed, Menzies and his government esteemed non-government schools not so much for their place in society as 'status symbols', but rather for their avowed mission to educate boys and girls in character as well as in learning.

As Prime Minister, Menzies frequently affirmed that the survival of freedom and democracy in a society such as Australia was dependent not so much on the efficiency of its government, or its economic prosperity, or even the strength of its defence forces but rather on the character and virtue of its own citizens. For Menzies, it was primarily the ethic of self-sacrifice and service to others that breathed fire into the life of democracy. Given that democracy represented a social contract of rights and responsibilities between citizens, it was the discharge of these responsibilities to one's neighbour that enabled democracy to flourish. It was precisely for their practical care and protection of others during the wartime blitz that Menzies lauded the besieged citizens of London as examples of 'fine democrats'. On the other hand, if people allowed the human predilection for self-interest to rule, Menzies warned that citizens would become 'tired democrats'. To overcome this fatigue, it was essential to inculcate in every individual, a spirit of service to the community and nation where the interests, wellbeing and comfort of one's neighbour would come first. Describing the capacity for self-sacrifice as a 'Godlike' quality, Menzies credited its inspiration to the Christian faith and the figure of Jesus Christ.

In addition to the cardinal virtue of selflessness, Menzies emphasised the supreme importance of tolerance as the great antidote to prejudice and hatred. For Menzies, tolerance was both a Christian ethic and a liberal principle of the Enlightenment. Menzies' concept of tolerance, however, did not necessarily resemble the contemporary, postmodern notion of tolerance as being merely an affirmation that all truth-claims, traditions, attitudes, habits and behaviours must be accepted as equally valid. To Menzies, such a definition of tolerance would no doubt have appeared to him as dogmatic, naïve and morally indefensible. What Menzies meant by tolerance was the capacity for human beings to understand one another and live peaceably with each another. It did not mean that citizens were compelled to validate or agree with the different belief-systems or lifestyles that others happened to embrace, but rather a mutual prepared-ness for people to understand, discuss and reason with each other's dif-ferences. In short, tolerance was about the freedom for individuals to agree to disagree.

With the ethic of tolerance presupposing a diversity of human traits and characteristics, Menzies saw human individuality as a quality to be af-firmed rather than suppressed. The uniqueness of every individual man and woman was a blessing and not a curse. In accordance with his lib-eral philosophy, he saw it as infinitely preferable for people to simply be themselves rather than seeking to be the 'same as everybody else'. If people had the freedom to be true to their individual personality and disposition, they could not only flourish as individuals but enrich the life of the community as a whole, with the disparate interests and occupations of citizens serving to complement each other. For Menzies, civil society represented one body with many parts, and the body could only function if each part discharged its own role. Thus individuality for Menzies was never a basis for separatism or the pursuit of narrow self-interest but rather a precondition for cooperation and the realisation of a truly con-tributory citizenship.

"The spirit of man can be touched to the finest issues; it can 'soar as a wild white bird, with a song unbound and fetterless', but it can never hope to do so if it is earth-bound by a mind which is groping in ignorance or blinded by prejudice and passion"
Robert Menzies, Freedom in Modern Society, 1935

"The most fundamental task in front of us is to educate a new generation, not for mere money-making or to comply with the law, but for an enlightened citizenship based upon honest thinking and human understanding"
Robert Menzies, Schools and the War, Broadcast, 16 October 1942

"The most important element in any new order...is not some plan that you work out on a sheet of paper or on a blackboard; the vital element in the new order will be the character of the people who live in this country."

Robert Menzies, The Individual in the New Order, City Hall, Brisbane, 21 January 1943

"It is not enough to be a rich country, it is not enough to be a prosperous country, it is not enough to have a superb system of industrial justice, it is not enough to have security, because not one of these things will distinguish us from the brute. It is what exists in the minds of men, in the spirit of men, that matters in a new world"

Robert Menzies, The Christian Citizen in a New Era, St Columba Presbyterian Church, Woollahra, NSW, 27 February 1944

"I know that every now and then you will meet men or women who are generally altruistic; but I say with regret that the majority of our citizens will approach the problem of politics with one question in mind – 'What will this be worth to me?' or 'What will I get out of it?'"

Robert Menzies, The Christian Citizen in a New Era, St Columba Presbyterian Church, Woollahra, NSW, 27 February 1944

"The great problems of mankind are not so easily disposed of because their causes are not to be found in the ingenious minds of lawyers but in the very vexatious hearts of men and women"

Robert Menzies, 'Address on Christianity and Law', St Stephen's Forum, 15 December 1946

"We become masters in this life by service. If we are to become masters we must first be servants. We can be the masters of the State only by being the servants and builders of the State."

Robert Menzies, Speech at Wesley Church, Melbourne, 4 September 1949

"Twice in this century men have died by the millions, largely because in what might have been the golden age of history men have learned to live with machines and have forgotten how to live with one another"

Robert Menzies, Election Speech, 10 November 1949

"In this great and free country of ours we have at least learned that hatred of other men is no instrument of progress but is merely a sign of decadence and despair"

Robert Menzies, Election Speech, March 1951

"The world needs something better than resignation, or cynicism, or the fading of great dreams, or the easy abandonment of great responsibilities. It needs courage and resolution and endurance and faith. It needs in particular that decent pride which gives to a nation or to a race a sense of destiny and continuity, a feeling deep in the heart that it stands for great things and that those things must not be surrendered or abandoned"

Robert Menzies, Broadcast on the Occasion of Australia's Jubilee Celebrations, 9 May 1951

"It is the glory of our democracy that the head of the Government is the servant of the people, not their master. It must be his constant duty to seek the good of all. If he is called upon to speak of the need for hard work, he must work hardest of all. If he urges a spirit of self-sacrifice, he must set an example"

Robert Menzies, New Year Message Broadcast, 2 January 1952

"How free and how democratic we shall be in this bright New Year will be decided by our own actions, the high and unselfish level of our thinking, our cheerfulness and good humour, and our sense of brotherhood"

Robert Menzies, New Year Broadcast, January 1953

"The most important thing in any centre of population is to develop a sense of community and of community service"

Robert Menzies, 'Australia Today – Man to Man', Broadcast, 11 November 1953

"You know as well as I do that the easiest and quickest way to score in a political argument is to appeal to intolerance, hatred and prejudice. Such appeals are, perhaps, good politics; but they are detestable statesmanship"

Robert Menzies, 'Australia Today – Man to Man', Broadcast, 17 March 1954

"Civilisation itself remains as something that resides in the human mind and the human spirit, and not something that can be turned on by a switch, or discovered in the roar of an aeroplane engine"

Robert Menzies, Freedom in Modern Society, 1955

"The test of civilisation is freedom, freedom of the spirit and of the mind and of the body"

Robert Menzies, Freedom in Modern Society, 1955

"If we want to raise our standards as a democracy, we want to get out of this habit of thinking that the main business of a democrat is to ask for things; and to come back to the plain truth that the main duty of a socially responsible democrat is to contribute to things, to give things, to hope that at the end of his life he will be able to say to himself without self-righteousness and without hypocrisy: 'I think I have put more into this community than I have taken from it".

Robert Menzies, Speech at Wesley Church, Melbourne, 4 September 1955

"When Churchill spoke about 'their finest hour', as indeed the younger Pitt might have spoken about it over a hundred years before, he wasn't talking about people who had, in the great trial of history, been taken up by their own desires, their own selfish interests, their own comfort. He was speaking of people who regarded sacrifice of comfort, the going hungry, the accepting of daily dangers, the helping of their neighbours under bombs and ruin of every kind, as their contribution to their country and to their race. They were great democrats"

Robert Menzies, Speech at Wesley Church, Melbourne, 4 September 1955

"The truth is, of course, that it is out of rivalry and generous emulation that the greatest development of our powers emerges. The history of the 20th Century abundantly attests that rivalry, ill-founded and basely considered, can breed envy and malice and hatred and uncharitableness. But an honest rivalry, a meeting on the merits, the matching of self-discipline against self-discipline, these are the salt of life"

Robert Menzies, Opening of Congress of the International Olympic Committee, Melbourne, 19 November, 1956

"I have travelled long enough and far enough to discover that there is something attractive in every land and that, if we could but get to know each other better, many of our problems would at once be seen to be artificial and would flutter away in the first wind of friendship"

Robert Menzies, Opening of Congress of the International Olympic Committee, Melbourne, 19 November, 1956

"We are always in danger of debasing our currency, not only in financial terms, but in moral terms, letting something become less warmly significant to us than it was before and the result is that there are thousands of people today who when they think of charity they think of it in terms of mechanics, of particular organisations, of social services, of all these great things that governments of any side today provide for the people as a matter of social obligation. These are not to be thought of as charity, and I'll tell you this, they are no substitute for charity, no substitute for love. You may hate your fellow man and still pay your taxes and provide him or help to provide him with an old age pension or a sickness benefit, and you may do all that hating him. You may be so poor that only to the most negligible extent can you do any of those things that the law requires of you and yet you may love your fellow man and so endow him with a great social wealth"

Robert Menzies, Farewell to Dr Rayward, Sydney, 30 March, 1958

"Charity is not a mechanical problem...don't let us get into the idea that we're great charitable people because by buying a ticket in a lottery and some charity gets the benefit at the other end. This has

nothing to do with charity, this has something to do with gain, with chance. Charity is not in a department, charity is in the heart and the mind of the individual person, nowhere else. We have no right to profess the religion that we profess unless we believe as our fathers before us believed that we have an individual responsibility that no third party on earth can take away from us"

Robert Menzies, Farewell to Dr Rayward, Sydney, 30 March, 1958

"The Apostle Paul wasn't talking about government departments, he wasn't talking about organisations, he was talking about something in the heart and in the mind of the person to whom he was writing, to the Corinthian, to whom he was speaking"

Robert Menzies, Farewell to Dr Rayward, Sydney, 30 March, 1958

"Why sir, is it that we are so proud, as I am myself, of this great matter of homes for aged people. It isn't because they're institutions, it's because they're not institutions. It's because they're homes, it is because they set out for the individual, the old man, the old woman living in them, not the sense of the institution like the old asylums one used to walk by as a boy, but a home, with friendliness in it administered with loving kindness, the maintenance of friendships, the sense of personal identity and of personal dignity. This is one of the great revolutions of our time that we should've been able to convert the old ideas into new ideas of an infinitely more Christian kind"

Robert Menzies, Farewell to Dr Rayward, Sydney, 30 March, 1958

"All that can be said about a Prime Minister is that he is the prime servant of his country. If he forgets that he becomes a menace, but if he remembers all the time that he is a servant of the country and is bound to produce what he believes is right for his own country, then people may vote for him"

Robert Menzies, Speaking at CTA Smoke Social, Melbourne, 9 August 1958

"I firmly believe that any man in public life who thinks that politics to him is just a job that will provide him with an income is making the most gross of all errors. The truth is that we must be the servants of the people, but in order to be the servants of the people, we are not to be servile, we are not to look at every problem and then say will this be popular or will this not be popular, because if that is the kind of leadership you're going to get, it will lead the country into disaster. It is not a matter of saying will this please somebody, it's a matter of saying is this the right thing to do if Australia is going to grow, if the country is to become richer and more powerful, if employment is to rise, if living standards are to rise and sir, that presents a problem which is a great challenge to many a man of character and honesty and imagination"

Robert Menzies, Speaking at CTA Smoke Social, Melbourne, 9 August 1958

"The whole art of civilisation is the art of learning to live with differences and of achieving a tolerance of other people's views, which is in reality one of the great threads of civilisation"

Robert Menzies, Address to Students at Gadjah Mada University, Jogjakarta, Indonesia, 3 December 1959

"Fear is our greatest enemy. So far, a century of the most brilliant scientific achievement, of growing political consciousness, of material advancement, has been marred by fear, suspicion, and actual hatred, to a degree without modern precedent"

Robert Menzies, Speech at Harvard University, 16 June 1960

"A man who does good because he expects thanks is committing a cardinal error. He must do good because he genuinely believes that it is a good thing to do. It is very agreeable if somebody says 'Thank you', but it doesn't always happen"

Robert Menzies, Pleasant Sunday Afternoon, Melbourne, 4 September 1960

"It was said once by an acute philosophic observer that there was a material difference between the Greek approach and the Hebrew approach. The Greeks placing a great premium on clarity of thought,

so much so that anybody who wants to understand the bases of elementary political thought and analysis will repair to the Greeks instantly to find the fountainhead, but the Hebrew tradition...has never concentrated simply on the quality of the mind, it has placed the first premium on the quality of conduct, and that after all, is an enormous contribution to make to the world"

Robert Menzies, Opening Speech at Mount Scopus College, Burwood Victoria, 13 September 1960

"This is a free country, and it's free in the best sense, meaning by that, that it believes in a just deal for everybody, it admires ability, it admires energy, but above all it admires decency. Character is by no means overlooked in Australia"

Robert Menzies, Opening Speech at Mount Scopus College, Burwood Victoria, 13 September 1960

"Pride is supposed to be one of the deadly sins. But pride in the sense of a proper self-respect, a determination to do your own work, and to play your own play, and to stand on your own feet – this is one of the great qualities in mankind"

R. G. Menzies, Speech at Cranbrook School, 10 December 1960

"It is a great quality to be independent, for a man to have a proper pride, and to say 'If I can do this myself I'm going to do it myself. And it is only if I can't do it myself that I must call on other people, if I have a chance, to help me to do it"'

R. G. Menzies, Speech at Cranbrook School, 10 December 1960

"The rarest form of courage, I think, in the world, is moral courage. The courage that a man has when he is prepared to form his view of the truth and to pursue it, when he's not running around the corner every five minutes to say, 'Is this going to be popular?'"

R. G. Menzies, Speech at Cranbrook School, 10 December 1960

"One of the great standards appears to be 'how much money does he earn? How much money does he laboriously accumulate?' I would like to say to my boys down there, I hope they don't succumb to that silly idea"

Robert Menzies, Speech at Knox Grammar School, Sydney, 15 December 1960

"And civilised minds are minds conscious of the past, aware of responsibilities of the future, and above all with standards in their minds, standards of faith, standards of the spirit that will enable them to avoid the bitter wretched paganism that has beset the world in the last 50 years"

Robert Menzies, Speech at Newington College, Sydney, 29 April 1961

"We must recapture our desire to know more, and feel more, about our fellow men; to have a philosophy of living; to elevate the dignity of man, a dignity which, in our Christian concept, arises from our belief that he is made in the image of his Maker"

Robert Menzies, The Challenge to Education, Address to Australian College of Education, 19 May 1961

"In life, the two great tasks of civilisation, which, if performed are the proof of civilisation, is that men should get to understand each other and value each other and be just to each other, and that they should be united in a brotherhood which is the inevitable result of the fatherhood of God"

Robert Menzies, St Joseph's College Sydney, 16 July, 1961

"You will test the civilisation of any community by finding out how many men and women there are in it who are prepared to do something, unselfishly, for other people"

Robert Menzies, Speech at Narrabri Town Hall Civic Welcome, 29 September 1961

"People who regard their work as a job achieve without difficulty a state of miserable mediocrity. The people who are going to do things properly must think that it is more than a job, that it is something that calls upon everything they have in them"

Robert Menzies, Opening of Medical Benefits Funds Building, Sydney, 7 October 1961

"It's a wonderful thing to see a man going along in life who has money, who has worked for it, who has accumulated some money, who finds his highest pleasure in giving it away; and giving it away in circumstances that will produce the maximum of pleasure

for as many people as possible,"

Robert Menzies, Opening of Cyril Rosenbaum Memorial Wing at Sir Moses Montfiore Jewish Home, Hunters Hill, NSW, 19 August 1962

"What we want in this country, what the world wants is a lot of people who are different, who are individual human beings, who have their own character and their own quality and their own ambition"

Robert Menzies, Springvale High School Speech Night, 12 December 1962

"There are a lot of people you will encounter who think that we all ought to be the same, that there ought to be a species of drab uniformity, that they all ought to be like me, so to speak, that they all ought to be like you, so to speak. This passion for uniformity is not to be encouraged"

Robert Menzies, Laying of the Foundation Stone at the Kew Jewish Centre, Melbourne, 25 August 1963

"A man may be tolerant because he is indifferent, because he doesn't care what happens to the other fellow, and so although it's good, it isn't everything. In reality what makes a contribution to a nation like Australia is the service of people who have enthusiasm and faith, who do believe in something. They are not tolerant because they are indifferent. They are tolerant because they have a passionate belief in their hearts"

Robert Menzies, Laying of the Foundation Stone at the Kew Jewish Centre, Melbourne, 25 August 1963

"For, if we are to be civilised people in truth as well as in name, we must be members of one another. For me, the perfect society would be one in which, by equality of opportunity and a full development of individual character and talent, each citizen was independent in his own heart and mind, but all citizens were inter-dependent in all social rights and duties"

Robert Menzies, First Baillieu Lecture, 6 July 1964

"Tolerance does not mean flabbiness. Tolerance does not mean that

we condone evil things or that we are not prepared to fight evil things. Tolerance is mutual understanding, forbearance, a desire to assemble ourselves every time there is a common cause to be served."

Robert Menzies, The Cardinal's Dinner, Sydney, 30 July 1964

"This capacity for sacrifice, this capacity for preferring other people to oneself, this capacity for saying, "I will contribute all if it is for the good of the country", exhibited so frequently in war is a God-like quality. The capacity for sacrifice, the whole idea of sacrifice is at the very root of the Christian faith"

Robert Menzies, Civic Service, Presbyterian Church, Cheltenham, 4 April 1965

"It's the supreme duty of every man to be unpopular in a good cause at some time or times in his life. If he is always popular it probably means that the he has run away from his problems half the time... Never be afraid to be different, because to 'Dare to be Wise' is to dare to be different"

R. G. Menzies, Address to Wesley College, 13 December 1965

"We in Australia have too much of a passion for uniformity. Everybody must have the same, everybody must go through the same kind of schooling, everybody if possible must have the same set of orthodox ideas. This is no good. The strength of a nation is in the differences that it has among its own people, so long as those are honest differences all serving a great ultimate national cause"

R. G. Menzies, Address to Wesley College, 13 December 1965

"Man is not civilised because he is clever, he is not civilised because he is a good chemist, he is not civilised because he is a good lawyer... but he is civilised if he has got to understand that he is living in a world of men and that he must understand men and be tolerant of men and stand for things that go beyond the bank account. That is civilisation and that is what we want"

Robert Menzies, Speech Day at King's School, Canterbury (England), 18 July 1968

"It can too easily be forgotten that a vital element in the great 'Battle

for Britain' was the courageous and serene and humorous quality of the people, men and women. This spirit, always latent, was evoked and inspired by him [Winston Churchill] as never before. He became, as I think I may have said elsewhere, a pillar of cloud by day and of fire by night"

Robert Menzies, 'The Science and Art of Politics', University of Texas Lectures (No 1), 20 November 1969

"In my declining years, witnessing a world in which moral values are treated with such complete contempt in some intellectual, or, more accurately, pseudo-intellectual circles, and in which the powerful influence of the Press seems to be, all too frequently, hostile to all received standards of social behaviour, I retain my belief in the ancient virtues, and value the services which the church schools and colleges render to them"

Robert Menzies, The Measure of the Years (1970), p 93.

"What is needed today is not some economists' theories but a great mood of unselfishness in our country, a great realisation in our country that unless we are prepared to be on the list of contributories, we can complain not a bit about other people who pursue purely selfish interests"

Robert Menzies, Conferral of the Freedom of the City of Kew, 11 August 1974

"You know, I think it was the Apostle Paul who said that 'we are all members [of] one another'...It means that no man lives to himself, that every man who lives in a community is a member of that community. He shares his membership with other people in it and, political friend or political foe, he owes them every good thing that he can contribute to the life of the country"

Robert Menzies, Conferral of the Freedom of the City of Kew, 11 August 1974

5

Fostering "a rugged honesty of mind": Menzies on Education

Winning scholarships to Ballarat's Grenville College and Melbourne's Wesley College, Menzies had appreciated the value of education and the life opportunities it offered from an early age. In adulthood, his faith in education was augmented by a liberal philosophy that esteemed education as one of the great driving forces of modern civilisation. For Menzies and other liberals, the power of education lay in its capacity to improve individuals thereby allowing them to bring a better world into being. Liberals saw education as having the potential to furnish individuals with the great faculties of reasoning, wisdom, sound judgment, moral character and religious faith which would equip them to become eminently better citizens. With his fondness of law, history and English literature, Menzies had a particularly intense belief in the merits of a humanities-based education, which in his words, enabled human beings to better 'understand their relationship with each other'. For Menzies, an education steeped in the humanities disciplines would ultimately ensure the survival of democracy in Australia. The humanities would help inculcate the virtues of moderation, decency and selflessness amongst Australia's citizenry, providing a healthy counter-weight to the vices of greed and selfishness that could all too readily stem from an emphasis on material progress alone.

The educational focus of Menzies was chiefly on universities with their long tradition of cultivating civilised minds. Far from functioning merely as utilitarian 'degree factories', Menzies saw universities as citadels of civilisation that would serve to build the character of their students and encourage them to seek the truth. Rather than standing aloof from the world, the university would bridge the gulf between the 'academician' and the 'good practical man'. In so doing, it would be in a position to contribute to the common good by producing an educated generation who understood the practicalities, values and aspirations of ordinary citizens. The other educational priority for Menzies was Commonwealth support for non-government schools which he esteemed as the great incubators of personal individuality and moral character. Eschewing a homogenous, one-size-fits-all approach to school education, Menzies maintained that a diversity of independent schools was necessary to tailor education to the individual needs of different children and their families.

As a graduate of the University of Melbourne himself, Menzies as Prime Minister was committed to advancing both the stature and scope of Australia's universities in the 1950s. In the post-war world, he envisaged these institutions as playing an ever important role in raising educated individuals to become the future leaders of Australian democracy. To facilitate the greater participation of Australian citizens in higher education, Menzies took steps towards the commonwealth funding of universities beginning with a scheme of undergraduate university scholarships inaugurated from the early 1950s. This initiative was followed by his establishment in 1956 of the Prime Minister's Committee on Australian Universities chaired by the British academic, Sir Keith Murray. Reporting on the state of universities in Australia, the 'Murray Report' recommended a tripling of Federal government funding for universities, emergency grants, significant increases in academic salaries, extra funding for buildings, and the establishment of a permanent committee, from 1961, to oversee and make recommendations concerning higher education. Within days of the Report's release, Menzies announced that he would implement virtually all of its recommendations. Under his leadership, the government inspired and supported an unprecedented expansion of education in areas that had traditionally been the preserve of state governments. New universities including the University of New England (1954), Monash

University (1958), Macquarie University (1964), La Trobe University (1964), the University of Newcastle (1965) and Flinders University (1966) were established placing tertiary education within reach of those who could not otherwise have had ready access. In the Press Conference immediately after his retirement as Prime Minister on 20 January 1966, Menzies cited his support for universities as one of his government's greatest achievements in domestic affairs.

In addition to supporting the consolidation of Australian higher education, Menzies and his government were committed to the flourishing of private education at the secondary and primary level. Menzies viewed religious education, of whatever tradition, as conducive to good character and good citizenship and given that many independent schools had a church foundation, he was keen for his government to financially support these institutions. With State governments failing to provide funding for non-government schools, particularly those in the Catholic system, Menzies took the first initiative to provide Commonwealth assistance to independent schools. Announcing an assistance package prior to the 1963 election, the Menzies government would fund science blocks for all schools and provide Commonwealth scholarships for senior students at independent high schools of all kinds. The funding for science would accomplish the material goal of aiding technological progress and national development while the scholarships would advance Menzies' objective of raising an educated generation of future leaders to run the country. In his retirement, Menzies reiterated the views he had expressed in 1943 that education of a religious nature was instrumental to cultivating the moral character of individuals who would one day assume responsibility for leading the nation.

As David Kemp appreciated, Prime Minister Menzies' reforms to both school and university education were guided by the vision that better education would lift the whole of society and the quality of every institution in it. It would improve leadership, it would improve public debate, and it would produce greater equality. Ever mindful of its far-ranging benefits, Menzies saw education as a means of promoting citizenship, personal development and social mobility, as well as boosting the national economy. The Australian educationalist, Dame Leonie Kramer, recognised the inescapable nexus between the political philosophy of Menzies and his approach to education, remarking that 'nowhere were Menzies' liberal-conservative principles better expressed than in his views about, and exceptional contributions to, education in Australia'. Kramer noted that 'so far as Menzies is concerned, education is the indispensable instrument in the promotion and protection of democracy'.

―――――――――――

"No society can confer the benefit of mental or spiritual freedom upon its members unless at the same time it encourages the search for truth and the fearless facing of the problems of the intellect"
Robert Menzies, Freedom in Modern Society, 1935

"If it is to be true that the truth lies at the bottom of a deep well, it is equally true that the well must be excavated"
Robert Menzies, Freedom in Modern Society, 1935

"The University must be a home of pure culture and learning. This was its original medieval function, and is still its first in order of real importance"
Robert Menzies, The Place of a University in a Modern Community, 1939

"Let me defend a so-called useless scholarship on the great grounds that it represents a sanity badly needed in an insane world; that it stands for a due proportion in life and living; that it develops the humane and imperishable elements in man; that it points the moral that the mere mechanics of life can never be the sole vocation of the human spirit"
Robert Menzies, The Place of a University in a Modern Community, 1939

"The work of research requires infinite patience, precise observation, an objective mind and unclouded honesty"
Robert Menzies, The Place of a University in a Modern Community, 1939

"The University must be a trainer of character...A man whose native impulses are good and whose instinctive standards are high will have his impulses touched to finer issues and the whole horizon of his life enlarged by the pursuit of higher learning"

Robert Menzies, The Place of a University in a Modern Community, 1939

"The University must be the custodian of mental liberty, and the unfettered search for truth"

Robert Menzies, The Place of a University in a Modern Community, 1939

"A rugged honesty of mind that does not shrink from the truth when it comes upon it in its path has always seemed one of the noblest of virtues; a glib dishonesty of mind which argues to a predetermined conclusion, determined in the light of passion or prejudice or selfishness, has always seemed to me the most contemptible of vices"

Robert Menzies, The Place of a University in a Modern Community, 1939

"Are the universities mere technical schools, or have they as one of their functions the preservation of pure learning, bringing in its train not merely riches for the imagination but a comparative sense for the mind, and leading to what we need so badly – the recognition of values which are other than pecuniary"

Robert Menzies, The Forgotten People Speech, 22 May 1942

"Above all, we shall need clear minds, honest minds, courageous minds, well-informed minds. In a word, educated minds. For the simple and unpalatable truth is that our democratic system cannot continue if its motive power is to be a mixture of class selfishness, materialism, disregard for minorities, and a somewhat lazy indifference to the future."

Robert Menzies, Schools and the War, Broadcast, 16 October 1942

"For the truth is that if education is to have any value to the individual it must represent a continuous process and not something which abruptly terminates when school days end."

Robert Menzies, The Future of Education, 19 February 1943

"One of the great functions of education is to produce critical minds in the best sense. Anybody who understands Australia and concerns himself with her future must have long since realised that if we could only substitute on a large scale critical minds for merely critical tongues we would go a lot further in a lot less time"
Robert Menzies, The Future of Education, 19 February 1943

"... the greater the facilities for post-school education, and the more continuous the interest of the citizen in the cultivation of the resources of his own mind, the more successful and intelligent will self-government become".
Robert Menzies, The Future of Education, 19 February 1943

"My own belief is that the maintenance of the Church schools, of whatever denomination, is so important – because a religious background for education is so important – that we must all be prepared to come together in the post-war world to devise ways and means of ensuring that those who are content with a purely secular education should be able to get it, while those whom such an education will never satisfy should be able to get the kind of training they want for their children without absolutely bankrupting themselves in the process."
Robert Menzies, The Future of Education, 19 February 1943

"The first function of education is to produce a good man and a good citizen. Its second function is to produce a good carpenter or a good lawyer, and the good carpenter and good lawyer will be all the better at their respective crafts if they have become aware of the problems of the world, have acquired some quality of intellectual criticism, and have developed that comparative sense which produces detachment of judgment and tends always to moderate passion and prejudice"
Robert Menzies, Education, Parliamentary Debates, House of Representatives, 26 July 1945

"The task of the teacher is one which brings him for hours every day, for many days, and for a number of years, into close contact with his pupils during their most formative years. It is a task which, if well performed, can do more to produce good citizens than all the acts of Parliament ever passed."
Robert Menzies, Education, Parliamentary Debates, House of Representatives, 26 July 1945

"The teacher does the work of making men. The physician and the surgeon can, at best, repair them; the lawyer can, at best, adjust their differences; and the engineer can, at best, provide them with the means of physical community association"

Robert Menzies, Education, Parliamentary Debates, House of Representatives, 26 July 1945

"An inadequately educated democracy is a contradiction in terms. We shall become perfectly democratic only when every citizen is given all the spiritual, mental, and physical training which he is capable of receiving"

Robert Menzies, Election Speech, 10 November 1949

"The University is the guardian of objectivity of mind: of the study of things on their merits, the study of truth as the truth, not merely to please anyone, but to serve the truth"

Robert Menzies, Speech on the Occasion of receiving an Honorary Doctorate of Laws at Sydney University, 29 August 1952

"Education does not simply mean the compulsory getting of a stock of knowledge. Knowledge is good; but wisdom is better. It is the way a man's mind works that matters. To be educated is to have learned how to think; to have acquired self-discipline; to have understood duty and the rights of others. These tasks are not merely scientific or mechanical. A man may be a great scientist, and be uncivilised. He may have mastered the technique of the law, but have no real understanding of its spirit. Education must produce a sense of values, high ethical standards, and a spirit of tolerance, or it fails"

Robert Menzies, 'Australia Today – Man to Man', Broadcast, 17 March 1954

"As the word implies, the University must not be narrow or unduly specialist in its outlook. It must teach and encourage the free search for the truth"

Robert Menzies, The Australian Universities, House of Representatives, 28 November 1957

"I hope that we will not, under current pressures or emotions, be tempted to ignore the basic fact that civilisation in the true sense requires a close and growing attention, not only to science in all its branches, but also to those studies of the mind and spirit

of man, of history and literature and language and mental and moral philosophy, of human relations in society and industry, of international understanding, the relative neglect of which has left a gruesome mark on this century"

Robert Menzies, The Australian Universities, House of Representatives, 28 November 1957

"Let us have more scientists, and more humanists. Let the scientists be touched and informed by the humanities. Let the humanists be touched and informed by science, so that they may not be lost in abstractions derived from out-dated knowledge or circumstances. That proposition underlies the whole university idea. It warrants and requires a great variety of faculties and the constant intermingling of those who engage in their disciplines"

Robert Menzies, The Australian Universities, House of Representatives, 28 November 1957

"We must, on a broad basis, become a more and more educated democracy if we are to raise our spiritual, intellectual and material living standards. Viewed in this way, our universities are to be regarded not as a home of privilege for a few, but as something essential to the lives of millions of people who may never enter their doors"

Robert Menzies, The Australian Universities, House of Representatives, 28 November 1957

"The Scientist is not to forget that natural philosophy cannot make its best contribution to life unless it is accompanied by a moral and mental philosophy which will give it balance...The great pure scientists, from Bacon to Newton to Rutherford, did their work in the atmosphere of intellectual liberation"

Robert Menzies, Address to the Tenth Session of the Australasian Medical Congress, Hobart, 5 March 1958

"As an instrument, science can achieve either good or ill. That will depend upon the minds and spirits of those who use the instrument"

Robert Menzies, Address to the Tenth Session of the Australasian Medical Congress, Hobart, 5 March 1958

"Psychologically, the true answer to the threat of war is to be found in the improving nature of man himself. Whatever we are called to do in the field of new and better satellites and ballistic weapons, we must not forget that the true function of science is to enlarge

the boundaries of human knowledge, and that of applied science to raise the standards of human living and happiness"

Robert Menzies, Address to the Tenth Session of the Australasian Medical Congress, Hobart, 5 March 1958

"It is the function of the University to offer not merely a technical or specialised training but a full and true education befitting a free man, a citizen of a free country"

Robert Menzies, Address to Convocation, University of Sydney, 28 August 1959

"A good university should be a guardian of intellectual standards and intellectual integrity. This, of course, involves a consideration of what has been called "academic freedom". There may be some who think that this expression connotes freedom from all restraints or from the normal rules which govern ordinary people. This is a misconception. "Academic freedom" connotes the absence of external or political compulsion upon the mind. It means that the search for truth must not be controlled by any authority other than the integrity of the mind and spirit of the searcher"

Robert Menzies, Address to Convocation, University of Sydney, 28 August 1959

"The greatest point about a University, is the quality of the mind and spirits that it produces. That is what counts in a University, that is why you have Faculties of Arts, that is why you study literature, or study history. Not because you are all going to be lecturers in English, lecturers in history, but because these studies broaden the mind, extend the horizons of the mind, and give a new freedom to the spirit of the student"

Robert Menzies, Address to Students at Gadjah Mada University, Jogjakarta, Indonesia, 3 December 1959

"When a man or a woman goes up to a University, he or she enjoys a degree of freedom and, therefore, a degree of responsibility that he or she never enjoyed before, and these matters impose great duties and the best way to understand them to realise that in learning the arts of these, in learning how to improve the prosperity of your country, to improve justice, as between human beings in your country, here is the place in which you have the opportunity of your lives to learn"

Robert Menzies, Address to Students at Gadjah Mada
University, Jogjakarta, Indonesia, 3 December 1959

*"The challenge to us as a nation is to play our part in increasing
the world's resources. And, in essence, that is a challenge to us
to improve our education; for it is only by constantly improving
education and skills that we discharge our world duty"*
Robert Menzies, The Challenge to Education, 1961

*"It still remains true that there is no higher education worth the name
unless it embraces not only the knowledge of physical science, but
the knowledge of mankind, the knowledge of the humanities, a
broad sweep of education, a broad and balanced training"*
Robert Menzies, Opening Westminster School, Adelaide, 13
February 1961

*"Whatever brand of politics the student may someday profess, or
reject, or ignore, the educator must look at him, not as an economic
unit someday to be recorded by a statistician, but as an individual,
to be sent out into the world someday as a better individual. For
the better the individual, the more conscious will he be of his
responsibilities to his neighbour and to society"*
Robert Menzies, The Challenge to Education, 19 May 1961

*"The main thing is that education must not be so resolutely utilitarian
as to be pagan and degrading. Secular education must not come to
mean selfish education"*
Robert Menzies, The Challenge to Education, 19 May 1961

*"I am convinced that if our approach to education is…"how much can
I get for myself out of it or how much can my family get out of it in
terms of financial advantage or social position?" then we shall see
the material advancement of the nation matched by moral decay,
and ultimately destroyed by it"*
Robert Menzies, The Challenge to Education, 19 May 1961

*"It will be a tragedy for Australia if, as a result of university
development, we don't produce, year by year, out of our universities
people who are not just qualified to earn a good income, but people
who have the heart of learning in their minds, who go on learning,
who have the scholar's habit even though they may be engaged in
some highly practical undertaking as the world would see it"*

Robert Menzies, Conference of Australian Universities, 17 August 1961

"Our great function when we approach the problem of education is to equalise opportunity to see that every boy and girl has a chance to develop whatever faculties he or she may have, because this will be a tremendous contribution to the good life for the nation, and to their own good life, because there's an immense personal satisfaction in accumulating some of the treasures of the mind. But we're never to fall into the error of thinking that we are all equal in talents, in aptitudes, in industry, in ambition, in energy, because if we are obviously not all identical, one or the other, in this way, it follows that what may be a very proper course of education for one may be inadequate for another, or inappropriate to a third"

Robert Menzies, Federation of Parents and Citizens' Associations of NSW, 1964 Annual Conference, 14 August 1964

"One of the great things that the university seeks to contribute to the world through its graduates is a sense of imperfection – not a sense of omnipotence – but a sense of imperfection, which is the sense that drives men and women into enduring intellectual effort"

Robert Menzies, Speech to graduates at degree ceremony, University of Melbourne, 26 April 1967

"To know how to learn and to wish to learn are the two greatest equipments [sic] that graduates can take away with them from a great university"

Robert Menzies, Speech to graduates at degree ceremony, University of Melbourne, 26 April 1967

"You can't be a good teacher unless you know how to learn. Then you will understand the people you are teaching, and their minds, and their outlook"

Robert Menzies, Speech to graduates at degree ceremony, University of Melbourne, 26 April 1967

"Every scholar should have a sceptical mind, for he must be constantly seeking the truth whatever the dogma may be"

Robert Menzies, Second Dunrossil Memorial Lecture, Melbourne, 12 March 1968

"For if education is to develop the mind of the individual student, then education becomes, however organised, an individual business, recognising the divine inequality of human beings in talent and character"

Robert Menzies, Sydney Grammar School Appeal, 13 June 1970

"The good teacher is not the one who sees a class as a mass or his own work as a job controlled by routine or rules, but the one who sees his pupils as individuals. They are not to be forced into one mould, but to be encouraged to expand and grow"

Robert Menzies, Sydney Grammar School Appeal, 13 June 1970

6

English Language and

Public Speaking

As an Anglophile and 'man of letters', Menzies had a profound affection for what he saw as the innate beauty and command of the English language. In his own use of English, his vocabulary was rich and his mastery of the language was polished. His love of English no doubt stemmed from his boyhood immersion in the great works of literature including the King James Bible, the plays of William Shakespeare, the poetry of John Keats and the novels of Charles Dickens. For rhetorical effect, his speeches frequently employed aphorisms and maxims from these classic works as a way of striking a cord with his audiences. To be sure, Menzies favoured the acquisition of a broad vocabulary but he preached and practised the virtue of simplicity in language. Frowning upon the unwieldy prose of modern 'bureaucratic-speak', he pointed out that the finest and most enduring pieces of English literature were peppered with words containing only one syllable. While Menzies was familiar with some Latin and French from his school and university days, he not so much aspired to be a classicist as a master practitioner of his mother tongue. Like Edmund Burke, he saw himself as owing a debt to the traditions that had been bequeathed to the present by his forebears, not least the English language. It was accordingly his responsibility, and those of the generations who followed, to steward the English language and cultivate its beauty for the enrichment of human civilisation. In his frequent addresses to school students, one of the key messages he was keen to impress on his young audiences was the need to cultivate good English. Menzies saw a proficient command of English as necessary for not only academic and professional success but also for social interaction and responsible citizenship.

One of the principal means by which individuals could develop and showcase their command of the English language was through the medium of public speaking, a craft Menzies himself cultivated to great effect from early adulthood. During his university years, extra-curricular participation in debating contests, addresses to the Historical Society and the fulfilment of his duties as president of the Students' Representative Council gave Menzies a taste of public speaking. The training in mooting and courtroom advocacy that Menzies received through his legal studies furthered his cultivation of the forensic art. His rapid advance in the legal profession was in no small part attributable to his recognised public speaking prowess as an advocate. Throughout his career, Menzies cared greatly about the art of speaking, whether in Parliament, to international gatherings or to more homely audiences, like those of the 'Pleasant Sunday Afternoons' in Melbourne's Wesley Church.

As Prime Minister, Menzies was eagerly sought after as a speaker to open new buildings, factories, hydro-electric works, lakes, fetes, shows, hospitals, schools, colleges and sporting events, and was in constant demand as an after-dinner speaker. Though a master of what he thought of as the science of government, Menzies also saw politics as an art, and talked of speaking as the acme of that art. Frederick Shedden, the Defence Department Secretary who worked closely with Menzies in both of his administrations and accompanied him to England in 1941, was one who saw lucidity as the secret of Menzies' success as a speaker in all settings:

His crystal-clear mind and beautiful English explain difficult things that worry the ordinary citizen, in such a manner that he [the citizen] feels they are the very things he has been feeling but unable to express himself.

A young Geoffrey Blainey was another who deeply admired the public speaking abilities of Menzies. Recalling his days as a pupil at Melbourne's Wesley College, the Australian historian offered this assessment of Menzies when he observed him speak at his Alma Mata:

He was the finest speaker I had heard – such eloquence, such timing, such a sense of the majesty of words, such a feeling for the occasion. There was a stately courtesy, which sometimes he even used when criticising opponents, though he was also capable of strong words delivered with mighty force. He had wit and a sense of fun: he could mock himself when the occasion called for it.

With his reputation as a fine public speaker, it was no surprise that the statesmen he most admired, including Edmund Burke, Abraham Lincoln and Winston Churchill, were each similarly remembered for their talent as orators.

Like Burke, Lincoln and Churchill, Menzies viewed public speaking as a critical tool to mastering the art of politics, for it was the power of speech that could not only communicate ideas but inspire the minds and hearts of people in a democracy. For speakers to effectively connect and engage with their constituencies, Menzies saw the authenticity of speech as paramount. For this reason, he tended to shun the modern practice of outsourcing speech-making to professional speech-writers. Instead, he preferred his words to flow directly from his own mouth and to formulate his speeches spontaneously from the podium using only minimal notes. The object of the speaker was always to move and persuade a contemporary audience. According to Menzies, the best way to do this was for the speaker to project their own personality in words which at least appeared to come fresh from their mind and lips. For the interest of the audience was piqued not by reading verbatim from a transcript but by the power and passion in the natural elocution of a speech.

Possessing a keen sense of history, Menzies also appreciated that it was the self-made speeches which would stand the test of time by virtue of both their oratorical quality and authenticity. Citing the example of Abraham Lincoln, he observed that if the President 'had not, on the way to Gettysburg, discarded the prepared speech and resorted to his own language, what he had to say would never have rung around the world or achieved immortality'. It was speeches, such as the Gettysburg Address, which would allow the future historian to perceive a past figure; whom they neither knew nor heard, through their own words. If the speech, however, was drafted by an anonymous speechwriter and not the statesman, 'the historian's light on the statesman becomes a little dim'. The historian would still be able to grasp the message and basic ideas in the speech written for the historical figure, but the important nuances of meaning and expressions of emotion would not be so apparent. In his self-made speeches such as his Forgotten People Address, the memorable turns of phrase and personalised style of Menzies was there for future historians to appreciate.

"English is, of course, not a dead language, but a living one. It must grow. It must put out new branches and twigs. But if it is to grow in strength and in beauty it must be from time to time pruned by the pruning knife of good taste and educated judgment"
Robert Menzies, Camberwell Grammar School Speech Night, 1938

"Lets us go back to simple, plain, honest spoken English. The English of the authorised version of the Bible, the standard of English which we have never approached since but which we might so easily recover if we all had not only knowledge of our language but a respect for it, a continuing knowledge of what it means and how it ought to be used"
Robert Menzies, Speech Day, Scots College, Sydney, 5 December 1953

"The great object of knowing your own language is to speak it with

justice and weight and simplicity"
R. G. Menzies, Speech at Cranbrook School, 10 December 1960

"Good speech, clear speech, speech which pays a just attention to the meaning of words is tremendously important"
Robert Menzies, Speech to the King's School, Sydney, 14 December 1960

"This is a wonderful language of ours. There is no language in the world that has such flexibility, that has such great literary stores in it, the greatest language of poetry that man has ever known, the great language of prose. It may lack some of the kick of French prose, but it is a marvellous language. It has contained some of the greatest writing, and some of the greatest speech in history"
Robert Menzies, Speech to King's School Sydney, 14 December 1960

"Let us respect this language. Don't let us have it broken down by all sorts of cheap importations — there are bound to be one or two. Let us respect this language. Because, I tell you that as you go through life, whether you are a lawyer, or a chemist, or a doctor, or a soldier, or whatever it may be, some element of your success, some aspect of your capacity to give expression to what you know, will depend upon your respect for the English language and your quiet command over it"
Robert Menzies, Speech to King's School Sydney, 14 December 1960

"Aim at simple, clear speech, and if you aim at that and achieve it, you will find that this will make a very great difference right through your lives"
Robert Menzies, Speech to King's School Sydney, 14 December 1960

"Correct English is the smallest debt we owe to the language that has been bequeathed to us by our forefathers"
Robert Menzies, Springvale High School Speech Night, 12 December 1962

"There are too many people who think it is good enough to talk out of the corner of their mouths... This is no good. Our language is, I believe, somewhat dogmatically, the greatest and most flexible language in the world. It is a marvellous language, and whatever you do in life, you will find that you can do it better and achieve better results in the doing of it if you can explain yourself to other people..."

Robert Menzies, Springvale High School Speech Night, 12 December 1962

"In this modern period of time, the capacity to communicate ideas is only less important than the capacity to evolve them. All the great scientists, all the great men of ideas would lose half their function in the world if they hadn't learnt to express themselves clearly and persuasively"

Robert Menzies, Opening of Haileybury College, 26 February, 1963

"You won't express yourselves in anything when you grow up and take on some task in life unless you have enriched your vocabulary and you enrich it by reading"

Robert Menzies, Opening of Haileybury of College, 26 February, 1963

"The art of speech is of course much admired. Its practitioners are numerous, for it is attractive. Its masters are few, for its difficulties are great. Yet it remains the most potent instrument for spiritual, social and political progress"

Robert Menzies, The George Adlington Syme Oration, Melbourne, 28 May 1963

"The work of the thinker cannot end in the laboratory or the study if it is to be fruitful for mankind. It must be conveyed to others clearly and, where possible, simply, in writing or in speech"

Robert Menzies, The George Adlington Syme Oration, Melbourne, 28 May 1963

"As I understand the matter, public or semi-public speaking has three main purposes; to instruct, to persuade, to entertain. The three are,

I hope, not mutually exclusive"

Robert Menzies, The George Adlington Syme Oration, Melbourne, 28 May 1963

"People are not roused and stimulated by the reading of an essay but by the passion and persuasion of a human being"

Robert Menzies, 'The Science and Art of Politics', University of Texas Lectures (No 1), 20 November 1969

7

Foreign and Defence Policy

At the same time as nourishing Australia's ties with Britain and the United States, Menzies and his government resolved to cultivate closer ties with Australia's Asia Pacific neighbours in the region he had identified in 1939 as Australia's 'near north'. Working with seven successive ministers for external affairs, from Henry Gullett to Paul Hasluck, Menzies would systematically expand Australia's diplomatic footprint in the Asia Pacific region, its aid to its neighbours, its trade with its neighbours, its education exchanges with its neighbours and, most critically, its military support for its neighbours. Shortly after Menzies' return to the prime ministership, his Minister for External Affairs, Percy Spender, set the tone for much of the government's ensuing approach to foreign affairs. In March 1950, he told the House of Representatives that Australia 'lives side by side with the countries of South and South East Asia, and we desire to be on good neighbour terms with them'. Representing this neighbourly approach of his government, Menzies paid official visits to several Asian countries, including India, Pakistan, Indonesia, Japan and Malaya between 1949-1966.

One of the first initiatives the Menzies government introduced to engage Australia more closely with Asia was the Colombo Plan. Under this programme of cultural and educational exchange, thousands of

Asian students became eligible to study at Australian universities. This provided an enduring link between Australia and future generations of Asian political leaders and business operatives. As John Howard observed, the experiences for so many young Asian students would prove vital years later in preserving the substance of Australia's bilateral relationships with its neighbours. The Colombo Plan was followed by the signing of the SEATO defence pact in 1954 which brought Australia into a partnership with not only the United States and European nations but Asian nations such as Thailand, Pakistan and the Philippines. During Menzies' second term as Prime Minister, his government established six new high commissions and embassies in South East Asia.

Supplementing these new cultural, defence and diplomatic ties with Asian nations, the Menzies government forged new trade relationships in the region with the most significant of these being the Australia-Japan Commerce Agreement of 1957. Despite Australia still reeling from the trauma of World War II, Menzies and his Minister for Trade, John McEwen pursued a trade relationship with the former wartime foe despite vehement opposition from the Labor Party and reluctance from the general public. Anticipating the Japanese appetite for mineral resources from Australia and elsewhere to fuel its rapid post-war industrialisation, the approach of Menzies and McEwen had been farsighted. The bilateral trade agreement struck with Japan in 1957 was followed by similar ones with Malaya in 1958 and Indonesia in 1959. The orientation of Australia towards Asia in trade policy under Menzies was reflected in the changing statistics of Australian imports. In 1949, 42% of Australia's exports had gone to the United Kingdom, with just 12% going to Asia. By the time Menzies left office in 1966, the percentage of Australian exports to the United Kingdom had fallen to just 17%, while exports to Asia rose to 31%. As the first Australian Prime Minister to officially visit Indonesia in 1959, Menzies remarked that Australia's 'relationships with South-East Asia are of tremendous importance to us' and urged Australia to always emphasise its points of unity in dealing with its Asian neighbours.

With the spectre of communism casting a shadow over the peace and security of the post-war world, the Menzies government practised a policy of 'forward defence' which it saw as the most responsible means by which Australia could contribute to peace and stability in its own region. If the ideals of freedom and democracy in the Asia Pacific region were to be protected from the threat of aggressive Communism, then Australia had an obligation to deploy its military forces to defend not only its own interests but those of its Asian neighbours. In several theatres of conflict including the Korean War, the Malaya Emergency, the Vietnam War and *Konfrontasi*, Australia executed its forward defence policy to assist its allies in the region to resist the march of Communism. Far from representing Australian attempts to impose the yoke of Western imperialism on Asian nations, Menzies and his government saw Australia's involvement in these battles as part of a broader mission to support millions of Asian people in their quest for liberty and independence. The forward defence of the Menzies government underpinned the 1954 SEATO pact through which Australia worked collaboratively with other South East Asian nations to defend democratic interests from Communist aggression. For all the merits of deploying military force, however, Menzies believed ultimately that the best resistance to communism lay not in the force of arms but in the inculcation of a spirit of freedom amongst the peoples of South Korea, Malaysia, Indonesia and Vietnam.

For Menzies, the deployment of forward defence to 'roll back' communism in South East Asia would not only give democracy the opportunity to flourish in the region but pave the way for even closer Australia-Asia relations. In 1970, Menzies commented that:

> ...given a satisfactory conclusion to the Vietnam War, Australia will be more and more occupied with the great tasks of establishing our relations with these countries on a basis of friendship and cooperation; with an increasing supply of technical assistance and financial and economic aid being provided by Australia

Thus far from simply ignoring Asia or viewing it suspiciously as a threat to Australian security, Menzies viewed the neighbouring region as ripe for cultivating friendly relations, providing the menace of Communism could be resisted and overcome. As Peter Edwards acknowledged, 'Menzies' relations with Asian countries, like those with his great allies, were far more complex and nuanced than various caricatures suggest'.

"In the Pacific we have primary responsibilities and primary risks. Close as our consultation with Great Britain is, and must be, in relation to European affairs, it is still true to say that we must, to a large extent, be guided by her knowledge and affected by her decisions. The problems of the Pacific are different. What Great Britain calls the Far East is to us the near north"

Robert Menzies, Broadcast Speech, 26 April 1939

"Japan is a country with which we were recently at war, and whose conduct of the war was such as to produce immeasurable bitterness among our own people. But we are now at peace. Are we to say that we will not trade with Japan?"

Robert Menzies, 'Australia Today – Man to Man', Broadcast, 16 September 1953

"You would at once agree that if we want to continue to be a great trading nation and maintain those exports which are our life-blood, we must be prepared to buy more things from Japan."

Robert Menzies, 'Australia Today – Man to Man', Broadcast, 16 September 1953

"The defence of the country is a task for all of us. We are not to grumble if the cost of this defence, either in terms of money or of personal inconvenience seems high. For if we lost our independent freedom, we have lost the whole foundation on which all spiritual, mental and physical freedom rests"

Robert Menzies, 'Australia Today – Man to Man', Broadcast, 23 April 1958

"In international transactions, the task of statesmanship is to get the best that we can without impairing the rights of other nations to have their own existence, their own future and their own pride"

Robert Menzies, 'Australia Today – Man to Man', Broadcast, 23 April 1958

"The most profitable thing, the thing calculated to do most good in the shortest time is to develop our personal and cultural relations with other countries. The economists may go on arguing, there will be hard-headed considerations of trade and finance and all sorts of other things when we get to other problems, but when it comes to human beings, we can't too soon begin to understand each other, to cultivate each other, to become friends of one another"

Robert Menzies, Speech at the Opening of International House, Melbourne, 14 May 1958

"It is a good thing that Australia should have earned a reputation for a sensitive understanding of the problems of people in other lands; that we should not come to be regarded as people who are detached from the miseries of the world. I know that we will not come to be so regarded, for I believe that there are no people anywhere with warmer hearts and more generous impulses"

Robert Menzies, Opening of World Refugee Year in Australia, 27 September 1959

"Today we know perfectly well that this great Republic of Indonesia lying there on the northwest of Australia is our greatest and most powerful neighbour, and we are interested in what goes on. Not interested in a protective or defensive way, but interested because we know that so many millions of people are managing their own affairs...Australia has a lively friendly warm interest in the development of Indonesia"

Robert Menzies, Speech at Dinner Tendered by His Excellency, First Minister Djuanda of Indonesia, 2 December, 1959

"The best thing that you can do for another country, if you are friendly with it, is to help it in the development of the people and the skills

which it will need"

Robert Menzies, Speech at Dinner Tendered by His Excellency, First Minister Djuanda of Indonesia, 2 December, 1959

"Our relationships with South-East Asia are of tremendous importance to us. It would be a misfortune if we were always to consider them in military terms...it is of the greatest importance that in our dealings with our Asian neighbours we should emphasise our points of unity and not dwell too heavily upon our possible points of difference"

Robert Menzies, Speech Marking Ten Years of Government, 10 December 1959

"It isn't philanthropy, but wisdom, to accept the task of guiding and helping other nations and peoples so that they may acquire, not only the institutions of freedom, but, much more importantly, those rising standards of living and of thought without which free institutions will wither and decay"

Robert Menzies, Speech at Harvard University, 16 June 1960

"If every nation in the world, which is now a free nation, decided that from now on it would look after itself - each for itself and the devil take the hindmost - the world would be tumbling into the most frightful catastrophe of history before we're 20 years older. The whole condition of survival is that the new nations should be made to feel that they have our sympathetic, individual interest, our desire to help, our desire to build them up"

Robert Menzies, Speech at the Opening of Legacy Week, 5 September 1960

"... we, the nations of the free world who enjoy prosperity, who can see in front of us a long vista of dramatically improving standards — must turn aside from time and have a look at our neighbour, though the neighbour may be five thousand miles away, and say: 'What about him? Is he coming along too?'"

Robert Menzies, Speech at the Opening of Legacy Week, 5 September 1960

"The two great achievements in foreign policy have been that we did get a three-cornered treaty with the United States of America and New Zealand in what is called the ANZUS Pact; and we also were one of the promoters of the South-East Asian Treaty which embraces in one defensive organisation not only Pakistan, and Thailand and the Philippines, and Australia and New Zealand, but also the United States of America, Great Britain and France.

These two are remarkable achievements, though I describe them in those terms myself. They have revolutionised the position of Australia"

Robert Menzies, Speech at Horsham, Victoria, 28 November 1960

"Communism is to be resisted not only by force of arms, though we must not shrink from that. It is also to be resisted by the developed character of people, by the building up of their own genuine belief in their own freedom, by the improvement in their own economy. It is to be resisted, as I said last year at a Council Meeting in Washington, by developing a sense of community which will translate the South-East Asia Treaty Organisation into a genuine community of self-interest, of self-reliance, and of mutual trust"

Robert Menzies, Statement at SEATO, 29 March 1961

"We shall defend ourselves in Australia, whatever the circumstances, to the very last gasp that we have, but we will defend ourselves with all the greater success if we know that we have great friends like yourselves who will be defending us or helping to defend us not because there is some statutory obligation, or not just because of some treaty between us, but because we both happen to believe in exactly the same things, the same attitudes of mind, the same patterns of behaviour, the same great attributes of character and quality"

Robert Menzies, White House Luncheon, Washington, 24 June 1964

"A great and civilised power must accept world responsibilities, must set out to discharge them, not priggishly, but with a real vision of what the world needs for the prosperity and happiness of its

people. In the performance of its duties, it will need patience and tolerance"

Robert Menzies, 'American – Australian Relations: What are they and Why?', Riecker Memorial Lecture Number 12, University of Arizona, 1967

"There is a notable tendency, particularly in this highly materialist world, to wish to live to and for ourselves, with our discreditable slogan, expressed with scorn in St Luke's Gospel: "Soul, thou hast much goods laid up for many years; take thine ease, eat, drink, and be merry". No such slogan can be adopted by a truly great nation. What it gives to the world will be the true measure of its greatness"

Robert Menzies, 'American – Australian Relations: What are they and Why?', Riecker Memorial Lecture Number 12, University of Arizona, 1967

"We have so great a duty to our neighbours, particularly our Asian neighbours, to assist them in the raising of their own educational, medical, scientific and technological development that we must take our part in finding or training our share of the expert minds that they need"

Robert Menzies, The Measure of the Years (1970), pp 89-90

"Our Foreign Policy was built around certain basic elements, and these were that we must be friendly and understanding with our neighbours in our corner of the world, but, if we should become involved in warlike operations, we should always be able to feel that we had great and powerful friends"

Robert Menzies, 'Looking Around at Eighty', Melbourne, 12 December 1974

8

History

At public occasions to honour the legacy of pioneers past, Menzies was fond of invoking the exhortation from the apocryphal Ecclesiasticus, 'Let us now praise famous men, and our fathers that begat us'. In Menzies' own eyes, history was pre-eminently about recognising one's place in the great procession of life that featured all of the towering figures who had come before. Of all the humanities disciplines, history was arguably the most instructive because its illumination of past causes and effects furnished statesmen, such as Menzies, with invaluable lessons for the present and future. Aside from appreciating history as a discipline in its own right, Menzies' enthusiasm for studying the past was no doubt reinforced by his early legal training with its focus on the Common Law doctrine of precedent. As a constitutional lawyer, Menzies understood that far from existing in a historical vacuum, the law was an ever-evolving institution that represented the augmentation of parliamentary statutes and case law over centuries. While always having to accommodate new developments and adapt to present-day circumstances to survive, the law remained informed by the dictates and conventions of the past. Thus in a similar vein, Menzies viewed human civilisation, more broadly, as the product of inherited customs and mores bequeathed from one generation to the next in the grand procession of history. The supreme value of history, according to Menzies, was that it gave human beings a sense of both tradition and continuity.

Given the myriad ways of interpreting human history, what was Menzies' own approach to making sense of the past? In the tradition of the nineteenth-century Scottish historian, Thomas Carlyle (1795-1881), it was evident that Menzies subscribed to a 'Great Man' theory of history that did obvious justice to the injunction of Ecclesiasticus. According to this interpretation, the historical course of nations such as Britain, the United States and Australia could be largely explained by the impact of highly influential leaders or heroes, particularly those in public affairs. Whether it was Edmund Burke, Abraham Lincoln, Alfred Deakin or Winston Churchill, Menzies esteemed these statesmen as figures of singular talent, industry, wisdom and political skill who had utilisedtheir power in a way that had a decisive historical impact. For Menzies, Burke and Lincoln represented the champions of modern liberty and democracy among the English-speaking peoples, Deakin was lauded as the 'great builder' for laying the foundation of Australia's national edifice and Churchill was revered for doggedly leading the defence of Western civilisation against the onslaught of Nazi barbarism. Regarding their respective legacies as incalculable and timeless, Menzies would have found it unfathomable for future historians to downplay the significance of these 'great men' in the historical narrative.

As a liberal of the English Whig tradition, Menzies also subscribed characteristically to the 'Whig' theory of history. According to Whig history, the past is portrayed as an inexorable march towards ever greater liberty and enlightenment, culminating in modern forms of liberal democracy and constitutional monarchy. While this view of history was popularised by the nineteenth-century historian, Thomas Babbington Macaulay, it had its roots in the thought of Edmund Burke. The eighteenth century Whig statesman held history to be primarily about the continuous growth and development of national life. Like Burke in the eighteenth-century, Menzies saw history as the chronicle of a nation's quest to improve its institutions, material comfort, science, art, literature and manners. Menzies, moreover, shared Burke's interpretation of English constitutional history as a slow and progressive realisation of 'the direct original rights of man in society' and of 'the balance of powers between the different interests in government, principally Monarchy and Parliament'. For both Burke and Menzies, these human rights had been progressively asserted and established in the growing canon of common and statute law in England. From his own grounding in English constitutional history, this was a historical tradition that Menzies was keen to nurture and advance in Australia.

With Macaulay building on the Whig precepts of Burke to craft his own historical narrative, his *History of England from the Accession of James the Second* (1848) waxed lyrical about the progress of England from the abyss of superstition and royal autocracy to the uplands of enlightenment and constitutional liberty. Subscribing to the Whig teleology of inexorable human progress, Macaulay enthused that 'the history of our country during the past hundred and sixty years is eminently the history of physical, of moral, and of intellectual improvement'. Macaulay's sanguine narrative evidently resonated with Menzies who quoted the august historian approvingly in his 1942 speech on *The Achievements of Democracy*. Like Macaulay in his time, Menzies observed that the preceding century had similarly represented 'a golden age in the improvement of the condition of mankind'. Menzies cited extensions to life expectancy, improved public health, the abolition of child labour and slavery, better education and the elevated status of women as proof that history was on an upward trajectory. Despite the intervention of two world wars serving to grievously disfigure modern civilisation, Menzies believed that it was Australia's destiny in the mid twentieth-century to continue the positive course Britain had charted in the previous century towards greater liberty and enlightenment. In this vein, Menzies saw history as providing the great stimulus for future reform and national progress.

Thus far from representing a merely academic specialty for intellectuals to indulge their curiosity, history for Menzies was an eminently practical discipline holding lessons for both statesmen and ordinary citizens to better understand the present. It provided a guide to identifying how the problems of the past arose and how they were accordingly dealt with. From studying history, national leaders could learn how to avoid the mistakes of their predecessors and employ wiser judgment in both decision-making and policy execution. Given the turmoil blighting the first half of the twentieth-century, Menzies regarded this purpose of history as paramount to realising a brighter, happier and more peaceful tomorrow. For civilisation as a whole, moreover, history could help sustain culture by reminding people of its origins, traditions and contribution to society over time. In his own study of history, Menzies appreciated the extent to which the Scottish culture of his forebears had enriched Australian life with its sense of rugged independence, humour and zest for education and learning. If a people, on the other hand, became amnesic about their heritage, then their culture would be in danger of stagnation and eventual extinction.

"If we fail to enjoy the present and the good things that are around us, we fall into the error of believing in the myth of 'the good old days"

Robert Menzies, 'Australia Today - Man to Man', Broadcast, 23 September 1953

"History is regarded by many people as somewhat old-fashioned. This is a basic error. History is not dead. We learn history not just so that we may quote dates and read the records of dead Kings, but so that we may consider how the problems of the past were dealt with and what errors were made and should be avoided"

Robert Menzies, 'Australia Today – Man to Man', Broadcast, 14 April 1954

"There are people who will tell you that the greatest revolution in history was the wheel. There are others who will tell you that the greatest revolution was light, the modern creation of light. There are those who will tell you today that the greatest revolution in human history has been brought about by splitting the atom. I venture to say to you, gentlemen, speaking in civilised terms, that the greatest revolution in the history of mankind was wrought when paper and printing became the common prerequisite of mankind"

Robert Menzies, Speech at Opening of Shoalhaven Paper Mills, 6 February 1957

"I know there are some people who think that tradition is rather a Tory invention. Tradition in any intelligent occupation in life is one of the great things that keeps it sweet and wholesome and influential, because tradition – national tradition, professional tradition, whatever they may be – these are the things that induce a sense of history and sense of proportion and sanity"

Robert Menzies, After Dinner Speech at Union House, Melbourne, 21 March 1959

"This sense of tradition, the sense of continuity – the feeling that one's predecessors have done well and one must not let them down – this is one of the great things in human life"

Robert Menzies, After Dinner Speech at Union House, Melbourne, 21 March 1959

"Indeed it is the greatest paradox of the 20th century that with all its superb cleverness it has been marked by more violence and hatred and barbarism than any other century since the Middle Ages"

Robert Menzies, Address to Convocation, University of Sydney, 28 August 1959

"It is the countries of the Western world who have been responsible for the biochemical improvements, for the antibiotic drugs, for the prolongation of life, for actively combatting disease, for doing all these things that have meant so much to men, women and children all over the world"

Robert Menzies, Opening of the McCaughey Institute, Corree, 19 November 1960

"There are millions of people in the world who looked out and saw Sputnik going across the sky who wouldn't have been alive to see sputnik if it hadn't been for the superb scientific work of Western scientists"

Robert Menzies, Opening of the McCaughey Institute, Corree, 19 November 1960

"I am an immense believer in continuity. I am not a believer in looking at the past because it is dead; but looking at the past because it is living; looking at the past because it reminds us that we are in the great procession of life. Any man who walked in the procession of life and who aims at doing anything in life, who is unaware of what went before him, unaware of the great truths that have come down to him, is a foolish man. He is essentially, a short-sighted man"

Robert Menzies, Speech at Newington College, Sydney, 29 April 1961

"The world would save itself from an abundance of errors if it knew something about human history. And we ourselves might get a more proper understanding of our opportunities in this world if we recalled a little history"

Robert Menzies, Citizens Luncheon, Ashfield Town Hall, 15 May 1961

"I am an immense believer in continuity. I believe that a sense of history, a sense of what has been done in the past and what may happen in the future does more to produce sanity of mind and judgment and stability of spirit than anything else"

Robert Menzies, Presentation at Hotel Australia, Sydney, 14 August 1964

"We must widen and deepen our knowledge of history, of human society, of the problems of man as a member of community and of the problems of other men living in other communities. For in a real sense, the world is becoming one world in which we must play a civilised and civilising part"

Robert Menzies, Second Dunrossil Memorial Lecture, Melbourne, 12 March 1968

"We do have some feeling, don't we, of responsibility for the future of the country and the future of human beings in it, and how can we discharge that responsibility unless we know something about our history, about what has gone on? Or are we so foolish as to believe that we sprang fully-fledged from the air and that history doesn't matter at all, that history is what we happen to make of it.

This is not true, we're in the great procession of history, there is no place in the world in which it can be better understood than it can be here, to know the past, not to dwell on the past, not to be smug about the past, but to know the past so as to derive inspiration from it, and pride, and standards from it, in the light of which, we propose to devote our activity to the future and to see that the future is worthy of the things generated in the past"

Robert Menzies, Speech at Dover College Luncheon, England, 12 July 1968

"To seek to abolish history is the ambition of a fool. For a land without history is a barren island in an uncharted sea. To tear up the roots is to destroy the tree"

Robert Menzies, Melbourne Scots – 'Father and Son' Night, 1968

9

Immigration and Australian Citizenship

Menzies and his government maintained and indeed expanded the Chifley Labor government's post-war immigration scheme established by Immigration Minister, Arthur Calwell in 1947. By the late 1950s, the ethnic composition of Australia had changed palpably with the influx of thousands of new immigrants from not only the UK and Ireland but also Poland, Hungary, the Baltic States, Germany, Italy and Greece, followed by arrivals from Lebanon and other parts of the Middle East. During Menzies' time as Prime Minister, however, the terms 'ethnic' and 'multicultural' did not surface in the political lexicon when discussing matters of immigration and citizenship. Rather, the phrase 'New Australian', coined by Arthur Calwell, was employed frequently to reflect the post-war policy of both Labor and the Coalition to assimilate immigrants into the mainstream of Australian life. It was held that this policy would best enable Australia to make the smooth and seamless transition from a largely homogenous composition to an ethnically mixed population. To facilitate the assimilation of immigrants, the Menzies government continued the Australian Citizenship Conventions (ACCs) and Good Neighbour Councils (GNCs) established by its Labor predecessors.

With Menzies and his government firmly committed to a policy of assimilation, what did this actually *mean* for new immigrants settling into Australian life? First, Menzies made it plain that the business of immigration and Australian citizenship was a 'two-way' street. Whilst new immigrants were expected to make every effort to adapt and contribute to their new homeland, there was also an obligation on the host country and its citizens to make these immigrants feel welcome. It was the responsibility of Australians to cast aside any inhibitions or prejudices they might have had to befriend and render practical assistance to newcomers in their midst. Although this was unfortunately not the experience for all immigrants, it was nonetheless a spirit that Menzies was keen to impress on his fellow Australians.

Second, assimilation for Menzies did not necessarily imply a rigid cultural conformity that served to suppress or erase all expressions of an individual immigrant's cultural identity. As a proud Scots-Australian himself, Menzies appreciated, first-hand, the importance for immigrants to cherish their cultural heritage and defended the many ethnic associations established in Australia for this purpose. What Menzies did object to, however, was the notion that ethnic communities in Australia should all dwell in separate ghettos where they existed merely as 'fractions' and not parts of 'one whole'. To be sure, Menzies' policy of assimilation aspired to build one Australia and one culture, but one infinitely enriched by the 'lively imaginations of thousands of people whose cultural background is remote from our own'.

If Menzies was open to Australia absorbing immigrants of different cultures and races, why therefore, did his government maintain restrictive immigration policies on the basis of race/nationality? Given Menzies' avowed Britishness, one obvious answer could be his suspicion and antipathy towards non-white races, but the evidence suggests otherwise. Dismissing the notion that Australia's existing immigration policy was based on racial superiority, he insisted that any such assumption was 'untrue, unjust and, indeed, absurd'. Rather, the most plausible explanation for this conservative approach is that Menzies believed a controlled immigration intake would give Australians optimal time to make sense of, and ultimately accept, social and cultural change by gradually changing the ethnic composition of the nation's population.

With the White Australia Policy representing a pillar of the 'Australian Settlement' since Federation, Menzies was well aware of the community maladjustment that the sudden removal of the policy could potentially cause. As David Kemp observed, Menzies knew that such pillars were too entrenched to be overthrown quickly, but could nonetheless be eroded over time. Conscious of the need for Australia to avoid the evident racial strife besetting some other settler-nations in the 1960s, Menzies was anxious to ensure that Australia's social cohesion would not be disrupted by any steep increase in the intake of non-European immigrants, many of whom he saw as inclined to form separate communities in societies such as the United States and South Africa. The most prudent approach, therefore, was to patiently convince the Australian people of the case for change through persuasion and incremental reform.

Thus while stopping short of repealing the *Migration Restriction Act*, the Menzies government enacted some reforms to relax the White Australia Policy. The Australian historian Neville Meaney pointed out that the 'R G Menzies' Liberal-Country Party government administered the restrictive policy somewhat more humanely and flexibly' than their Labor predecessors under Chifley. Menzies' first minister for immigration, Harold Holt, permitted 800 non-European refugees to stay and admitted Japanese war brides in 1949. The following year, the introduction of the Colombo Plan allowed Asian students to study at Australian universities. In 1957, the government allowed non-Europeans who had been resident in Australia for fifteen years to apply for naturalisation and admitted some 'distinguished and highly qualified non-Europeans for indefinite stay'. The government allowed Australians to sponsor Asian spouses for citizenship in 1959 and in 1964 the conditions of entry for people of non-European stock were eased.

The two most significant attempts to modernise immigration and citizenship policy under Menzies were the abolition of the 'dictation test' and the introduction of the Nationality and Citizenship Bill, both in 1958. In May 1958, Menzies' Minister for Immigration, Alexander

Downer (Snr), introduced the Migration Bill to remove the dictation test. Introduced by the Barton government in the first years of Australian Federation, the dictation test had allowed the government, at the discretion of the minister, to block unwanted migrants by forcing them to sit a test in 'any European language'. As Downer noted, the dictation test had 'been used to prevent the entry to Australia of both Europeans and Asians, and also as a means of deporting people within five years of their arrival, even though they were legally admitted to settle permanently'. Denouncing it as one of those 'singularly ugly museum pieces of the Victorian age', Downer argued that the dictation test was 'out of keeping with the ideas of the second half of the 20th century' and claimed that its discriminating effect had 'evoked much resentment outside Australia', 'tarnishing our good name in the eyes of the world'. In its place, the Menzies government introduced a simplified and expedient 'entry permit' for new arrivals.

Desiring to place naturalised Australians on the same footing as Australian-born people in relation to loss of citizenship, the Menzies government introduced the Nationality and Citizenship Bill in August 1958. Immigration Minister Downer told parliament that the Bill would make 'Australian citizenship' a 'one-class train, without any suggestion of first or second class according to origin'. Articulating the approach of the Menzies government to immigration and Australian citizenship, Downer lauded the legislation as 'another example of the Government's determination to absorb, not by compulsion, but by opportunity, our new settlers into Australian customs, traditions, privileges, and rights'. He told parliament that 'we shall only succeed in this great movement of peoples from the old world to our own continent if we acclimatise them, and their children, sympathetically and speedily to our ways of living, and induce them to regard Australia as their home'.

Contrary to the perceptions of some historians and political commentators, the philosophy behind the immigration policy of Menzies and his government, especially in its latter years, was not so much one of forcing new arrivals to conform to Australian cultural customs and mores but rather one of giving immigrants the maximum degree of freedom and ease to become Australians. The policy essentially proceeded from the reasonable premise that in their human quest to participate and belong, new immigrants to Australia were intrinsically disposed to adopt, without external pressure, the prevailing customs, values and traditions of their new homeland. In short, Menzies believed that immigrants were drawn to Australia for what it was and not for what they desired it to become.

In his approach to immigration and citizenship, Menzies was neither a white race exclusivist in the tradition of Billy Hughes nor a multiculturalist in the mould of Malcolm Fraser but a realist patriot who favoured voluntary assimilation as the best path for immigrants to become part of Australia. Unlike earlier Australian Prime Ministers such as Edmund Barton, Billy Hughes and Stanley Melbourne Bruce, Menzies did not regard Australian citizenship and national identity as being the sole preserve of the white British race. In Menzies' Australia, immigrants of non-British extraction would be encouraged to become Australians in the fullest sense and no longer be excluded from national life as foreign 'outsiders'. Whilst demonstrating a more liberal attitude towards race, however, Menzies like his predecessors remained essentially wedded to an Australian identity defined pre-eminently by a British cultural paradigm.

Although immigrants in Menzies' Australia would be free to retain their cultural traditions, there was also the expectation that they would embrace the Australian 'host culture' comprised of such British-derived staples as the English language, the monarchy, democracy and the rule of law, the Judeo-Christian tradition, community-centred volunteerism and the ethic of liberal independence. With Menzies regarding this British cultural legacy as superior to that of other civilisations, it made eminent sense for 'new Australians' to embrace this as their own. Unlike many of his successors who championed Australian multiculturalism, Menzies did not hold to the modern premise that all cultures were necessarily equal and valid. While it perhaps appears dated and ethnocentric to modern sensibilities, Menzies saw the policy of encouraging immigrants to assimilate to a set of received Australian cultural values and traditions as inherently sensible and justified during his time.

"Every one of us in this country is either a migrant himself or the descendant of one. We therefore of all people should be prepared to welcome into our community all those who can by their work and citizenship contribute to the strength of this land"

Robert Menzies, Election Speech, 20 August 1946

"Though we naturally want as many migrants as we can get of British stock, we denounce all attempts to create hostilities against any migrant or group of migrants, whether Jew or Gentile, on the grounds of race or religion. Once received into our community, a new citizen is entitled to be treated in every way as a fellow-Australian. The strength and history of our race have been founded upon this vital principle"

Robert Menzies, Election Speech, 10 November 1949

"If every one of us in Australia understood that migration was vital to our existence, growth and development, that we should regard every migrant as our friend, and we should go to no end of trouble to make every migrant feel at home"

Robert Menzies, Prime Minister's Speech at First Citizenship Convention, 1950

"While recognising the need to promote immigration we have always had two things in mind. The first is that new settlers coming here should not remain in separate groups or colonies but should be absorbed into Australian society and life. The second is that the volume of migration should be regarded flexibly and should be adjusted from time to time to our economic conditions"

Robert Menzies, Immigration, Broadcast, July 1953

"A great immigration programme, getting people into this country while they are available to be got, people who will bring into the national life of Australia all the variety of ideas and of histories and of cultures that will so strengthen this country when it grows to full maturity"

Robert Menzies, Speech to Young Liberals, Melbourne, 1 April 1957

"All parties have cooperated and all sections of the community have cooperated...in supporting this great enterprise [of postwar immigration] ... Making those who have come to make their lives in this country, feel that they are indeed members of this country, making them feel at home, making them feel that from now on they are Australians, sharing with us our joys and sorrows, our privileges and duties"

Robert Menzies, Opening of the Citizenship Convention in Canberra, 22 January 1958

"We are having our culture enriched by the lively minds and the experiences and the lively imaginations of thousands of people whose cultural background is remote from our own. These are wonderful things, and on balance, I believe they have been doing great things for Australia"

Robert Menzies, Opening of the Citizenship Convention in Canberra, 22 January 1958

"That is the great work of migration, building a nation...if you are building a nation, you must have long views not short ones... to build a nation requires the acceptance of difficulties and their overcoming, the acceptance of risks and the putting of them into their proper place"

Robert Menzies, Opening of the Citizenship Convention in Canberra, 22 January 1958

"Let us pride ourselves on having a broad, high conception of the destiny of our country and you can't do that politically if your politics are all based on little bits of selfishness and little bits of prejudice and little bits of class distinction and setting one person against another. We have no reason for existence as a Party, and I have no reason for existence as its leader, unless we can truthfully claim unity and for the highest ideal and the broadest sweep of national citizenship"

Robert Menzies, Liberal Party Rally, Cottesloe (WA), 8 March 1958

"New citizens do not come here from overseas just because for the time being we want them to come. They come because, like the grandparents and great grandparents of so many of us, they want to come; because they are attracted by life here with its adventure and its ambitions and its hopes"

Robert Menzies, 'Australia Today – Man to Man', Broadcast, 19 March 1958

"It is our national desire to develop in Australia a homogeneous population in order that we may avert social difficulties which have arisen in many other countries"

Robert Menzies, Statement on Australian Immigration Policy, Honolulu, 9 May 1959

"So far as I know, most nations have policies which determine the intake of citizens from other countries. So far as Australia is concerned, I want to make it quite clear that our policy, to which the overwhelming majority of Australians are deeply attached is not based upon any idea of racial superiority. We willingly recognise that citizens of other nations possess abilities and traditions which we sincerely respect and admire. When, therefore, a citizen of some Asian or Oriental country is refused permanent entry to the Australian community, it is not because we are assuming to ourselves some superior quality. That would be untrue, unjust and, indeed, absurd"

Robert Menzies, Statement on Australian Immigration Policy, Honolulu, 9 May 1959

"We are in fact a friendly people, not given to making distinctions among people on grounds of race or religion. But we do not want to see created in our country minority problems or prejudices or occasional bitterness such as exist in some countries where large numbers of non-Europeans and Europeans live in separate communities"

Robert Menzies, Statement on Australian Immigration Policy, Honolulu, 9 May 1959

"The truth of the matter is that all the great races and great nations in the world have been built up upon aggregating a variety of people, and acquiring from each variety a quality which matters.

This has been a great, great thing in the history of Australia. I hope that we will all resist...any idea that we should be put out into separate fractions and pretend that we are just fractions, and that we are not really parts of the whole"

Robert Menzies, Speech to the All Nations Club, 25 November 1960

"One of the great beauties of what has been happening in Australia is that the thousands, and now becoming hundreds of thousands, and growing into millions, of people who have come here from overseas, they are not isolationists...On the contrary, they come here, knowing by all their background and experience, that we become more and more part of the world, part of the world of thought, part of the world of literature, part of the world of music, part of the world of painting and of sculpture. And all this will tend, in Australia, to make us a more internationally minded community"

Robert Menzies, Speech to the All Nations Club, 25 November 1960

"We have believed, and believe, that the flow of good people, with a variety of cultures and experiences, and backgrounds into this country is giving to us a strength, a vigour, a variety of minds which we would never otherwise have acquired. We believe that a large movement of immigration into Australia is of the essence of national development"

Robert Menzies, Liberal Party Rally at Wayville, South Australia, 13 February 1961

"I think it is a very good thing that we from time to time remind ourselves of our inheritance, but it would be a bad thing indeed if, in a country like this, racial communities tended to separate themselves out. The great thing about building up Australia through a programme of this kind is that we should become one people"

Robert Menzies, Citizenship Convention, 23 January 1962

"What we need in Australia is that every person coming from some particular race or faith who comes into the Australian

community should retain his quality in that sense but should add it to the qualities of all the other people in the community so that finally we get a powerful structure, a self-respecting structure, a community of high ideals and of clear faith and of generosity and of understanding"

Robert Menzies, Laying of the Foundation Stone at the Kew Jewish Centre, Melbourne, 25 August 1963

"In the years since World War II, Australia's immigration programme has brought to this country people from all parts of Europe with a diversity of historical and cultural backgrounds. Many of these people were refugees from oppression. Many derived from happier circumstances. This flow of new citizens has played an important part in building the nation. It is something which has given us great satisfaction and we wish to see it continue. However, it is basic to our immigration policy that all these new citizens should be integrated as fully, and as quickly, as possible into Australia's national life"

Robert Menzies, Speech on Yugoslav Immigrant Organisations, Ministerial Statement, House of Representatives, 27 August 1964

"We do not expect newcomers to turn their backs on their original heritage. On the contrary, it is wholly understandable that immigrants should establish organisations amongst themselves for a variety of social and cultural purposes. It rather follows the precedents of the Irish and Scots in this country. These organisations, as honourable members will know, can also be a most valuable means of assisting migrants to become fully integrated into the Australian community"

Robert Menzies, Speech on Yugoslav Immigrant Organisations, Ministerial Statement, House of Representatives, 27 August 1964

10

Law and the Constitution

Despite Menzies' career as a young man at the Victorian Bar having been superseded by forty-years on the political stage, he remarked in his 1967 memoirs, *Afternoon Light,* that 'the practice of the law in court was and remains my first love'. His years in parliament had failed to dim the fond memories he held of the law with its 'joys of forensic advocacy, the fine petillant flavour of cross-examination, the thrust and counter-thrust of argument, the quirks and quiddities of individual judges and opponents, the rich occasions for humour, the whole arresting pattern of oratory' and the 'fierce but bloodless battles between "learned friends"'. The law and the institution of the Bar, in particular, provided Menzies with the first great opportunity to cultivate and exhibit his considerable faculties of logical reasoning, speech-writing, oratory, advocacy, wit and humour, all of which would come to define his reputation as a consummate parliamentarian. In his 2004 Sir Robert Menzies Memorial Lecture, the then Attorney-General, Philip Ruddock, reminded his audience that 'when we think of Menzies' abilities as a politician, it is easy to forget what a good lawyer he was'.

From Menzies' early adulthood, a successful career in law appeared eminently promising. Gaining entry into the School of Law at the University of Melbourne in 1913, Menzies' distinguished academic performance attracted a string of prizes. Reflecting his evolving interest in Constitutional law, Menzies won the Dwight Prize in British History and Constitutional History in 1914. This was followed in 1915 by the John

Madden Exhibition in Jurisprudence and the Jesse Leggatt scholarship in Roman law, the law of contract and the law of property. In his final year, Menzies published his award-winning essay, *The Rule of Law During the War* (1917), with an introduction by the Melbourne University Professor of Law. After graduating from the University of Melbourne with First Class Honours, Menzies was admitted to the Victorian Bar and to the High Court of Australia in 1918. Establishing his own practice in Melbourne, Menzies specialised chiefly in Constitutional law which he had read with the leading Victorian jurist and future High Court judge, Sir Owen Dixon. Dixon not only became his pupil master but became his life-long mentor. Dame Pattie once had to remind Menzies that 'Dixon is not God' to which Menzies retorted 'Yes, but only just'.

As a junior advocate, Menzies made his first appearance in the High Court in a case, *Troy v Wrigglesworth* (1919), where he appeared before a full bench of five judges. The case concerned a Commonwealth employee, an army driver, who had been caught speeding in St Kilda Road, Melbourne. Menzies conducted the appeal of this driver before the full High Court Bench and three of the five judges ruled in his favour. Even one of the two dissenting judges, Gavan Duffy, told Menzies that 'he had been very impressed by the ability with which you presented your argument'. In that case, he recalled appearing before Sir Edmund Barton, Australia's first prime minister who was then still serving on the bench until his death in 1920. He observed that Justice Barton 'had a fine brown and a lambent eye, a great natural dignity, and admirable capacity for good living, a not extensive technical learning in the law, but a sound legal approach, a human but scholarly mind'. In 1920 Menzies served as an advocate for the Amalgamated Society of Engineers which eventually took its appeal to the High Court of Australia. The case became a landmark authority for the positive reinterpretation of Commonwealth powers over those of the States. The High Court's verdict raised Menzies' profile as a skilled advocate. Appointed a King's Counsel in 1929, Menzies regularly appeared in the Victorian Supreme Court and in the High Court.

Following his entry into Victorian State politics in 1928, Menzies served as the Victorian Attorney-General between 1932 and 1934. After transferring to Federal politics in 1934, Menzies became Commonwealth Attorney-General in the Lyons government. His period as Attorney-General was focused on constitutional issues. Menzies appeared in the Privy Council in the famous case of *James v Commonwealth* which concerned the Commonwealth's ability to regulate the marketing of dried fruit. Acting for the Commonwealth, Menzies submitted that section 92 of the Constitution, dealing with the freedom of trade, commerce and intercourse among the States, did not apply to the Commonwealth. Although his case was unsuccessful, the Privy Council acknowledged 'the appreciation of the help given to them by [the] Attorney-General for the Commonwealth, the merit of whose admirable argument is in no way diminished because it has not succeeded'. The most significant constitutional issue to arise during his period as Attorney-General was the crisis arising from the abdication of King Edward VIII in 1936. With Menzies describing the circumstances as 'remarkable and unprecedented', parliament was recalled to pass a special resolution to assent to the alteration of Australia's succession laws. As Ruddock noted, this required some skill as Australia was yet to adopt the Statute of Westminster and Menzies needed to explain the difficult constitutional position which prompted the resolution.

Menzies' experience at the Bar and his political career as Attorney-General gave him an abiding understanding of the Australian Constitution and an appreciation of its relationship to politics. As Prime Minister, he came to regard the Constitution as the most fundamental and sacred of all laws to which the parliament was its servant. As such, he regarded any changes to the Constitution as a matter never to be entered into lightly, a sentiment shared by the Australian people in their typical wariness to assent to changes proposed by a referendum. From the defeat of the September 1951 referendum proposing a constitutional amendment to outlaw the Communist Party, Menzies learned that getting 'an affirmative vote from the Australian people on a referendum proposal is one of the labours of

Hercules' with the ordinary voter disposed to vote 'No' when in doubt. Accordingly, Menzies held that any constitutional changes proposed needed to be 'crystal clear' to avoid giving rise to either 'misinterpretation or absurd fears'. Given the predilection for the electorate to vote 'No', the greater onus was on the proposing side to make the case for changing the Constitution.

Like that of the electorate at large, the approach of Menzies to constitutional reform was generally conservative but this did not mean he necessarily viewed the Constitution as static. From his experience as a counsel in the *Engineers Case*, he appreciated that the Constitution was capable of evolving without any formal amendment. They included changes in methods of interpretation by the judiciary and the reinterpretation of old powers in new ways that would not have been envisaged by the constitutional drafters. As a pragmatist, Menzies accepted the needs for the Constitution to change by interpretation to meet the practical demands of the day. Appreciating Menzies' expertise in both the theory and practice of constitutional law, Sir Paul Hasluck reflected that the Prime Minister was a 'constitutionalist in philosophy and debate' who understood the character and scope of Australia's supreme body of law.

As well as the Constitution, the other great pillar of Australian jurisprudence that Menzies cherished was that of the common law. Formulated over centuries by judges, courts and tribunals in England, this body of case law precedents was received into Australian jurisdictions through the *Australian Courts Act* (1828). Thereafter, the English common law gradually evolved into Australian common law with its accretion of fresh precedents from the new Australian courts. As a young barrister, Menzies was steeped in the common law with his practice specialising in not only constitutional law but also family law, contracts, property law and wills. In his familiarity with the common law, Menzies could see the genesis to so many of the basic individual rights and freedoms that would form the bedrock of his liberal philosophy. He admired the common law for its inductive method of moving from precedent to precedent, an approach he saw as not only well-grounded but eminently prudent and practical. Like the monarchy, the common law for Menzies was a British tradition that had evolved over centuries of history with an inherent genius to adapt to modern times. As Prime Minister, neither his proficiency nor interest in the law waned as his legal skills of statutory interpretation and advocacy proved critical to his success as a parliamentarian. It was a tribute to Menzies that in 1964 when Dixon retired as Chief Justice of the High Court, some thirty years after Menzies had been in active practice, both Dixon and Barwick thought that Menzies was the man to take over as Chief Justice.

"The judiciary is in my opinion the most important element in our institutions of liberty. Without an independent or authoritative judiciary liberty would become a mere name"

Robert Menzies, Attorney-General of Victoria, 'The Machinery of Government', 1928-29

"If there is one thing that emerges from our whole constitutional history it is this – that the genius of our nation has been expressed in an elaborate system of checks and balances, of balancing one power against another power, in order that by a balance achieved by the whole of them tyranny on the part of any one of them may become impossible"

Robert Menzies, Attorney-General of Victoria, 'The Machinery of Government', 1928-29

"Of all laws, that of the Constitution is at once the most fundamental and the most sacred. Parliaments may tell us from day to day what we are to do or not to do. The Parliaments themselves are controlled by the Constitution, which is not their servant but, on the contrary, their master"

Robert Menzies, The Law and the Citizen, Broadcast 3AW, 12 June 1942

"The Commonwealth Constitution is the organic law under which the Commonwealth Parliament and the Commonwealth Government

are set up and exercise their functions. Neither parliament nor government can alter it. Only the people can do that. They were its creators forty years ago. They are its masters still"

Robert Menzies, The Law and the Citizen, Broadcast 3AW, 12 June 1942

"In modern times there has been a considerable passion, particularly on the part of some of my Brethren of the Law who have occupied high office in various parts of the British World, for putting things into writing. This notion is, I believe, contrary to the whole genius of our people. We don't live under codified laws and we have always distrusted codified ideas. There is nothing truer than that 'the letter killeth'"

Robert Menzies, Constitutional Guarantees, Broadcast 3AW, 27 November 1942

"Laws are useful things. But no law can improve the spirit of man; no order can be a substitute for a strong will; no government can do for us what...we cannot or will not do for ourselves"

Robert Menzies, New Year Message Broadcast, 2 January 1952

"In Australia, we have a wonderful record of honest administration of the law. There has been no hint of corruption among our judges. There have been high standards of skill and industry and impartiality. Many great leaders of the Bar have sacrificed the greater portion of their incomes to serve on the Bench, where their contributions to judicial law, and the authority of the law, and the popular confidence in the integrity of the administration of justice, have been of supreme value"

Robert Menzies, 'Australia Today – Man to Man', Broadcast, 10 March 1954

"If a government wants to amend the Constitution, it is practically essential to have the support of the Opposition"

Robert Menzies, The Measure of the Years (1970), p 119

"The common law is, I think, the greatest contribution that the English genius has made so far in the history of the world. It exhibits all the

genius of the English and of ourselves in the inductive method of moving from precedent to precedent, of not being dogmatic about something, not being codified but proceeding on a basis of the common law and its superb inductive methods"

Robert Menzies, Australia-Britain Society Inaugural Dinner, Sydney, 26 August 1971

"When we, in Australia, come to discuss civil and political rights, it is necessary to remember that one of the functions of the Common Law, devised over a course of centuries in England and adopted by us by inheritance, has been to protect the individual against infringement of his personal rights"

Robert Menzies, 'Civil and Political Rights', Article for Melbourne Herald, 13-15 March 1974

"To live in a Common Law country is, in itself, the very best guarantee of the rights of the individual"

Robert Menzies, 'Civil and Political Rights', Article for Melbourne Herald, 13-15 March 1974

11

Liberalism

The key to understanding the liberal philosophy of Menzies is to appreciate it in its historical context, duly recognising it as the Australian heir to a long tradition of English Whig liberalism nurtured by Edmund Burke, T B Macaulay and William E Gladstone with roots in the seventeenth-century natural rights precepts of John Locke (1632-1704). In short, it was a philosophy of personal freedom, enterprise and progress that cherished the time-honoured traditions that had given it its birth. Menzies' former colleague and Governor-General, Sir Paul Hasluck, accurately observed that Menzies saw himself as the philosophical legatee of Gladstone, the Victorian British liberal statesman and four-time Prime Minister.[1] Drawing his political inspiration from the liberalism of nineteenth-century England, Menzies regarded himself as the custodian of a humane and reforming liberal creed which he desired to revive and adapt to the twentieth-century Australian context. Originating from the old Whig party of the earlier nineteenth-century, the English liberals had an enviable record of sponsoring humane social reforms to advance the cause of individual dignity and freedom. With the support of some Tory parliamentary colleagues, Whigs and liberals achieved Catholic Emancipation in 1829, *the Reform Act of 1832* to broaden the franchise, the abolition of slavery in 1833 and the progressive abolition of child labour in British mines and factories.

When Menzies took the word "liberal" for his new political party in

1944, he consciously assumed the mantle of the old English liberals to realise the same ideals of individual dignity, freedom and opportunity for his own people in his own time. Although Menzies did admire Alfred Deakin and his earlier generation of Australian liberals, he believed that Deakinite liberalism had entertained a somewhat over-optimistic view of the state and its capacity to regulate the economy, the workplace and society.[2] Accordingly, he sought to re-orient liberalism in Australia to its first principles of respect for the individual, personal and community responsibility, and the encouragement of enterprise. [3] As Menzies resurrected his political career, he had found the opportunity to further develop and promulgate his liberal philosophy in a series of radio addresses that became known as *The Forgotten People*. Menzies himself described *The Forgotten People* collection as 'a summarised political philosophy'.[4] Representing the blueprint of his liberal philosophy, *The Forgotten People* encompassed a wide range of topics including Roosevelt's Four Freedoms, the future of capitalism, the nature of democracy and especially the role of the middle class, 'the forgotten people' of the title and their importance to Australia's future as a democracy. The addresses frequently emphasised the values which Menzies regarded as critical to shaping Australia's wartime and postwar policies. These were essentially the principles of liberalism: individual freedom, personal and community responsibility, the rule of law, parliamentary government, economic prosperity and progress based on private enterprise and reward for effort.[5]

Seeking to lead his country once again, Menzies and his new Liberal Party campaigned on this philosophical platform in the 1946 and 1949 Federal elections. The Liberal leader's promise to free individuals and families from socialist state controls resonated with the Australian electorate who elected Menzies as Prime Minister in December 1949. As a liberal Prime Minister he successfully re-established the concept of a limited role for government, kept taxes in check, eschewed extensive new schemes of regulation and centralisation and encouraged free enterprise.[6] Unlike his counterparts in Britain and New Zealand, Menzies did not take Australia down the path of nationalisation of private industry by compulsory acquisition or cradle-to-grave welfare.[7] During his long reign, Menzies never wavered in his conviction that liberalism was pre-eminently conducive to national progress. In his election campaign speech of 1958, Menzies explained how the application of liberal principles would bring not only material dividends, but spiritual and mental benefits as well, serving to make a great nation even greater.

While the liberalism of Menzies was focussed on the dignity and freedom of the individual, the unit of the individual by no means represented an end in itself. On the contrary, nourishing the wellbeing of the individual was the primary means to realising the common good of society. In his 1964 speech to the Liberal Party's Federal Council, Menzies told his audience that it was by realising that 'men and women are not just cyphers in a calculation, but are individual human beings' that his government was able to achieve positive outcomes for society such as industrial justice and peace, the provision of social services to combat poverty and the distribution of housing to raise general living standards.[8] Menzies never regarded people as atomistic individuals existing for their own self-interest and preservation but as members of a society possessing rights and duties. Far from espousing a self-serving liberalism preoccupied with hyper-individualism, material greed or mere pleasure-seeking, the liberal creed of Menzies was essentially self-giving with its emphasis on the freedom of the individual to serve others and contribute to the common good without the compulsion of the state.

With individuals existing as interdependent members of one society, the liberal creed of Menzies rejected the politics of division. Emphasising the rule of law and the equal dignity of all citizens, his liberalism repudiated both the Marxist doctrine of class warfare and the old prejudices of sectarianism, racialism and nationalism that had plagued Australian society since the colonial years. Instead of perpetuating these divisions, Menzies sought to promote a political culture of civility, inclusiveness and mutual understanding between citizens of different regions, classes, races and faiths. For Menzies, a liberal government must be capable of transcending the politics of sectional interest to deliver policies and programmes for the good of *all* Australians, whoever they were and wherever they lived. According to David Kemp, his policies in health and education, and the openness of his Liberal Party to people of all faiths succeeded in dissipating decades of religious hostility in Australia between Catholics and Protestants. In essence, Menzies' election pledge to govern not only for those Australians who had voted for him but also those who voted against him was an expression of his liberal creed.

"I wonder if we always realise that, when we shrink from the arduous labours of thought and abdicate the responsibility of judgment in favour of somebody else, we to that extent make ourselves slaves to somebody else. The formal homage and slave's collar of early feudalism have gone, but there will always be a feudalism of the mind as most of us are prepared to live in a state of intellectual villeinage"

Robert Menzies, Freedom in Modern Society, 1935

"We must avoid the common fallacy of supposing that freedom and discipline are inconsistent...The discipline we must look for is not the discipline of the slave, but the discipline of the volunteer. Such discipline does not take the form of a compulsory obedience to a higher authority, but is based upon an intelligent understanding of the fact that order and sanity are essential if the liberty of the individual is to be reconciled with the rights of other individuals"

Robert Menzies, Freedom in Modern Society, 1935

"One of our most highly developed arts appears to be that of transferring our burdens to somebody else's shoulders. There was a time (or so I imagine) when misfortunes tended to drive a man inwards, on to his own resources; a process which developed fortitude and ingenuity, the two great qualities which go to make up the pioneering spirit"

Robert Menzies, Freedom in Modern Society, 1935

"My protest is against that false humanitarianism which does not strengthen but corrupts; which does not rest upon the view that I am my brother's keeper, a view which is the noblest embodiment of the Christian philosophy, but rests upon the belief that my brother should be my keeper, and that I should leave my troubles to him"

Robert Menzies, Freedom in Modern Society, 1935

"... the choice is not between an unrestricted Capitalism and a universal Socialism. We shall do much better if we keep the good elements of the Capitalist system, while at the same time imposing upon Capital the most stringent obligations to discharge its social and industrial duty"

Robert Menzies, Has Capitalism Failed? (Broadcast), 7 August 1942.

"The old conservative doctrine that the function of the State was merely to keep the ring for the combatants has gone forever; the grim picture...of a Capitalist system in which there is unrestrained and cruel competition, in which employees are sweated and workers treated like cattle no doubt had some truth in it – and still has too much to satisfy humane minds. But we have learned a great deal about how to use private enterprise for our own social and national ends"

Robert Menzies, Has Capitalism Failed? (Broadcast), 7 August 1942.

"A modern and civilised Capitalism has much to contribute to the post-war world"

Robert Menzies, Has Capitalism Failed? (Broadcast), 7 August 1942.

"The best and strongest community is not that in which everybody looks to his neighbour hoping for something from him, but that in which everyone looks to his neighbour, willing and able to do something for him. In brief, we achieve the good of man when we help and encourage him to be a man – strong, self-reliant, intelligent, independent, sympathetic and generous"

Robert Menzies, The Task of Democracy, 13 November 1942

"The man who is, in fact, his own master will scarcely need to have on the wall a list drawn up by himself of things which he must not do"

Robert Menzies, Constitutional Guarantees, Broadcast 3AW, 27 November 1942

"I have never believed that a virile and independent and really liberty-loving community can be built up if the habit is developed regarding social benefits as something handed out by the Government and paid for by other people. 'Contribution' means self-respect. It destroys any suggestion of charity. It means that the citizen is paying his own premium towards his own insured protection"

Robert Menzies, Social Security after the War, Broadcast, 4 December 1942

"The greatest fallacy that can be put into people's minds and, indeed, the greatest deception that can be practised upon them is to be found in the view that private enterprise can be destroyed and social conditions improved at one and the same time"

Robert Menzies, Social Security after the War, Broadcast, 4 December 1942

"If we are all to make some reasonable advance there must be not a mere redistribution of the world's goods but a marked increase in the world's goods. In other words, progress is essential to the elimination of poverty"

Robert Menzies, Social Security after the War, Broadcast, 4 December 1942

"Our democratic system has exhibited far too much evidence of social injustice and human insecurity; but its underlying disease, of which the other things are merely symptoms, is the disease of selfishness and irresponsibility. If a new material order, or an improved material order is to serve the highest needs of mankind, it must be accompanied by a moral revolution which will make every citizen feel that the wellbeing of his country is his own responsibility, that he is his brother's keeper, and that his stature as a citizen will depend far more upon what he gives than upon what he gets"

Robert Menzies, Social Security after the War, Broadcast, 4 December 1942

"...the enterprise of the citizen, who desires to get an extra reward for doing some extra good job. That, I believe, is still one of the most vital driving forces in human nature..."

Robert Menzies, The Individual in the New Order, City Hall, Brisbane, 21 January 1943

"If we are to use private enterprise, individual initiative, the capitalist system if you like...then we must say...Look if you are to have the right to ask for a reward, then you must submit to the obligations that are brought about when you enter a civilised community in which the government accepts responsibility for the weak and the unfortunate"

Robert Menzies, The Individual in the New Order, City Hall, Brisbane, 21 January 1943

"So we must say to capitalism, to private interests, to the employers of Australia – 'You are a vital element in this new world, but you must be prepared as a condition to meet your obligations, to pay the highest wages that your industry can bear, to provide civilised working conditions for your people, and to provide constant employment for as many people as possible."

Robert Menzies, The Individual in the New Order, City Hall, Brisbane, 21 January 1943

"The individual in a democratic land, and I say this to you deliberately, is not only the creator of the national character, he is its repository. It is on him that all responsibility rests."

Robert Menzies, The Individual in the New Order, City Hall, Brisbane, 21 January 1943

"I do not believe that the average young Australian looks forward to a life in cotton wool"

Robert Menzies, The Individual in the New Order, City Hall, Brisbane, 21 January 1943

"You cannot make a good community out of bad men. You cannot make an active community out of lazy men. You cannot make a courageous and independent community out of dependent men. The idea that you can have a lot of soft and flabby individuals who take no responsibility and make no contributions and that you can build a real nation out of them is all utter nonsense."

Robert Menzies, The Individual in the New Order, City Hall, Brisbane, 21 January 1943

"Businesses, if they are to provide secure employment, must be permitted and indeed encouraged to be profitable, that is, to be successful. But in a just world no business can be allowed to be successful except on terms that it pays proper wages, that it affords civilised living conditions, that it contributes adequately to the social security of its employees, that it stabilises employment as far as possible, and that it admits its employees to the greatest possible extent to some share in the benefits which it may yield as a result of their cooperative effort."

Robert Menzies, Opening Speech, Camberwell Town Hall, 23 July 1943

"So far from it being wrong to endeavour to secure a material margin in life, it is in my opinion the great, solvent and stable element in proper society. Profit enables savings, thrifty people are the repositories of that spirit of individual independence and ambition which is the motive force in a progressive society."

Robert Menzies, Opening Speech, Camberwell Town Hall, 23 July 1943

"However much and however humanely Parliaments and Parties may labour for the elimination of poverty and disease and unemployment, it will always remain true that our greatest asset and our greatest security will be found in virile and independent manhood"

Robert Menzies, Social Security, Broadcast, 17 September 1943

"If we stand for anything as Liberals we stand for the inescapable responsibility of the individual, his dignity, his significance, his responsibility for every other individual. In that sense we are an individualist movement, not in the bad sense of saying, 'Each for himself and the devil take the hindmost', but in the good sense of saying that every man is his brother's keeper"

Robert Menzies, Speech at the conclusion of the Albury Conference, 16 December 1944

"The more absorbed the people become in the technique of material living, the more they have neglected their social responsibilities, and the more, unhappily, they have neglected the problems of self-government."

Robert Menzies, Education, Parliamentary Debates, House of Representatives, 26 July 1945

"It is therefore to the preserving of the freedom of the citizen, his mind, his body, his spirit, that Liberalism dedicates itself. Only from genuinely free, progressive, diligent and encouraged individuals can a really powerful nation be built"

Robert Menzies, Provisional Policy Statement, 31 August 1945

"Shall we, as the Labour Socialists desire, carry forward in perpetuity the war system which subordinates the individual to the mass and seeks salvation, not through the divine restlessness and ambitious enterprise of the individual, but through the growth of Departments and the multiplication of rules and regulations? Or shall we build upon Liberal democracy, which passionately believes that the war was fought to overthrow the authoritarian state; that there can be no national progress except through the

efforts of the individual; that life should be free and its horizons wide"

Robert Menzies, Election Speech, 20 August 1946

"The first answer to this foul doctrine of the 'class war' is to do all we can in a positive way to show both employers and employees that they work in a common enterprise, in which neither can succeed without the other, in which each should share in prosperity, in which the employer's greatest asset is a body of contented employees who feel that they are understood and fairly treated, and the employee's greatest asset is a successful business which can guarantee to him steady employment and expanding opportunities"

Robert Menzies, Election Speech, 20 August 1946

"We aim at high wages; good conditions; friendship in industry; sharing of prosperity; the independent settlement of differences by Conciliation and Arbitration; the protection of the rights of employers and employees by the law; the enforcement of the law; the rejection of anarchy"

Robert Menzies, Election Speech, 20 August 1946

"The Liberal Party looks first and foremost to the natural elements in a progressive society and seeks to encourage them. The answer to the evils of bureaucracy is not more bureaucracy — but a restoration of that full individual activity and full industrial production which will raise the level of employment and of prosperity much more safely and certainly than a merely negative approach."

Robert Menzies, Election Speech, 20 August 1946

"Let us produce our way to prosperity. Instead of treating individual enterprise and special skill and ambition and the search for reward, and thrift, and independence as if they were the enemies of a dull and dreary uniformity, let us recognise them for the friends and servants of us all. Liberalism brings to you the only real hope of a free, friendly, prosperous, and growing Australia"

Robert Menzies, Election Speech, 20 August 1946

"It must be remembered that there is a constant struggle going in the heart and mind of man – a struggle between his instinct for liberty and his more primitive instinct to exercise power over another man, to show himself the better man of the two"

Robert Menzies, Freedom and the Call to Action, Lecture to Junior Chamber of Commerce, 4 August 1947

"When we speak of freedom we are not speaking of something which is absolute in its terms. Absolute freedom for every individual would deny the existence of the State and would equally deny all community life, the basis of which is that the individual abates some of his own freedom in favour of justice to his neighbour and reasonable degree of freedom for all"

Robert Menzies, Freedom and the Call to Action, Lecture to Junior Chamber of Commerce, 4 August 1947

"One of the great freedoms in this life is the freedom to have some choice of occupation and, not liking it, to change it for another."

Robert Menzies, 'Bond or Free', Wesley Church, Melbourne, 7 September 1947

"There is another freedom which is under challenge today, and this is a very important freedom, because without it our immortal souls will be in deadly peril. It is the freedom to do our best and to make that best better. This is a great freedom. Here we have a freedom that goes deep into every dignity of man. Freedom to do your best; to give of that best so that in the long run that best becomes even better"

Robert Menzies, 'Bond or Free', Wesley Church, Melbourne, 7 September 1947

"The virtue of competitive private industry is not that it makes profits for individual employers but that it ensures freedom for the citizen and benefits for the customer, and a varied life for all"

Robert Menzies, "The Liberal Leader Speaks: Socialism", Weekly Broadcast, 12 August 1949

"The more we can encourage men and women to be skilful and industrious, by incentive payments, by reasonable profits, by the encouragement of thrift and saving, the more we help them to look

*to themselves and not just to leave it to the Government, the better
the State will be says the Liberal"*

Robert Menzies, "The Liberal Leader Speaks: Employment",
Weekly Broadcast, 26 August 1949

*"The best people in this community are not those who 'leave it to the
other fellow', but those who by thrift and self-sacrifice establish
homes and bring up families and add to the national pool of savings
and hope someday to sit 'under their own vine and fig-tree', owing
nothing to anybody"*

Robert Menzies, Election Speech, 10 November 1949

*"The real freedoms are to worship, to think, to speak, to choose, to be
ambitious, to be independent, to be industrious, to acquire skill, to
seek reward. These are the real freedoms, for these are of the essence
of the nature of man."*

Robert Menzies, Election Speech, 10 November 1949

*"In a sense quite different from the one in which Karl Marx used it,
I believe that the world does belong to the workers. That is, rising
social and material standards in Australia"*

Robert Menzies, "Australia – Man to Man", Broadcast, 2
September 1953

*"It is foolish to seek to divide Australia into employers and employees
as if their interests were diametrically opposed"*

Robert Menzies, 'Australia Today – Man to Man', Broadcast,
17 March 1954

*"I am one of those simple minded, old-fashioned people, who believe
that an honest business, courageously conducted with enterprise
is, in itself, a great service to mankind. If it were not for the men
of commerce in our race, we would today be the least of God's
creatures in this world"*

Robert Menzies, Speech at the Associated Chamber of
Commerce, Menzies Hotel, Sydney, 22 November 1954

*"Now, we believe in profits because they both reward and encourage
enterprise. We are against profiteering, but think that the best answer*

to it is to encourage more and more free enterprise and competition"

Robert Menzies, General Elections 1955: Taxation on Company Profits, Broadcast, 17 November 1955

"The marks of prosperity in a country are high employment, high standards of housing, high wages, high profits and a high tide of national and industrial development."

Robert Menzies, General Elections 1955: Taxation on Company Profits, Broadcast, 17 November 1955

"A great and efficient and well-organised productive enterprise earns good profits because it pays good wages and provides continuous work and has contented employees. And in turn those employees have high wages and good conditions and assured jobs because they are working for a profitable and expanding business"

Robert Menzies, General Elections 1955: Taxation on Company Profits, Broadcast, 17 November 1955

"We in Australia have been thought worthy of the confidence of entrepreneurs from other countries and that we have received into this country, capital, people, skill, the great traditions of long-established businesses and that out of them all, we're in the course of building a country so powerful that a few occasional adverse winds are not going to reduce it to misery or frustrate its course"

Robert Menzies, Opening of De La Rue Factory, Sydney, 14 March 1958

"Well-considered and properly planned public works and private works are to be thought of not in terms of rivalry but in terms of cooperation for the advancement of the nation"

R. G. Menzies, 'Australia Today – Man to Man', 9 April 1958

"As I believe that what matters in a country, far more than butter or eggs or milk or cheese or wheat or wool, is freedom, the freedom of the mind, the freedom of the spirit, then we are to do nothing that will put those great things at risk"

Robert Menzies, Address to Apex Club Luncheon, Hotel Terrigal, 19 April 1958

"Competitive enterprise – a state of affairs in which a man's skill and personality will produce better results than in the case of a man without skill and without personality. That, I think, is very good. The competitive element is one of the great secrets of stability in the country"

Robert Menzies, 71st Annual Association Day Banquet at the Commercial Travellers' Association of NSW, 13 August 1960

"This is, I think, a very remarkable community effort. There is a lot of self-help in this matter; and there is some help by the Government. Now that is as it should be. We must marry these two elements together."

Robert Menzies, Official Opening of Goodwin Homes, Canberra, 22 July, 1961

"The guarantee of liberty and the guarantee of character is to have true individual citizens who think for themselves, who have had their minds developed, who have put themselves in the way of learning more and more right through their lives and are therefore able to speak their minds and resist any petty aspiring dictator in whatever field who may come along to them"

Robert Menzies, Address to Launceston Church Grammar School, 18 September 1961

"A Liberal regards this country as having only valid class distinction, the distinction between the active and the idle"

Robert Menzies, Young Liberal Movement Convention, Sydney, 27 July 1962

"If Liberalism stands for anything, and young Liberalism above all, it's for a passion to contribute to the nation, to be free but to be contributors, to submit to the discipline of the mind instead of the ordinary, dull discipline of a regimented mass of people"

Robert Menzies, Young Liberal Movement Convention, Sydney, 27 July 1962

"You can't build up an independent nation on a foundation of dependent people. The spirit of independence, this fire that burns in the veins of an independent nation must burn in the veins of

the individual. We cannot succumb to the ideas of our opponents which, roughly, are that whatever good is to be done must be done by that mystical being the Government. This is a matter for the individual; this is a matter which calls for a spirit of adventure, a desire to contribute"

Robert Menzies, WA Convention of the Liberal Party, South Perth Civic Centre, 30 July 1962

"As the etymology of our name "Liberal" indicates, we have stood for freedom. We have realised that men and women are not just cyphers in a calculation, but are individual human beings whose individual welfare and development must be the main concern of government"

R. G. Menzies, Speech to Federal Council of the Liberal Party, Canberra, 6 April 1964

"We have learned that the right answer is to set the individual free, to aim at equality of opportunity, to protect the individual against oppression, to create a society in which rights and duties are recognised and made effective. In this free society, the tyrannical notion of an all-powerful State is rejected and dogmatic Socialism with it. In its place, we have put opportunity without any class privilege, social and economic justice, and the civilised democratic conception that governments are not the masters of the people, but their servants"

R. G. Menzies, Speech to Federal Council of the Liberal Party, Canberra, 6 April 1964

"Rising material standards of life in a democracy cannot be adequately attained unless industries are developed, production increased, and the resources of the nation expanded. They will not be attained by a simple process of redistribution, nor by the creation of a state of affairs in which we are all employed by and dependent upon the State"

Robert Menzies, First Baillieu Lecture, 6 July 1964

"The truth is that if in the long run the best thing is to be done for the most people, then this is not just a matter of dividing up what exists, but a matter of adding to what exists"

Robert Menzies, Address to Liberal Party of Australia (NSW), 7 October 1964

"We have learned that true rising standards of living are the product of progressive enterprise, the acceptance of risks, the encouragement of adventure, the prospect of rewards. These are all individual matters. There is no government department which can create these things"

Robert Menzies, Afternoon Light, 1967, p 282.

"Liberalism in Australia is not to be defined by looking at a Policy Speech or a political platform. The thing to remember constantly is that Liberalism is an attitude of mind and of faith, aiming at the highest standards of life, both material and spiritual"

Robert Menzies, Inaugural Sir Robert Menzies Lecture, Perth, 12 May 1970

"We prefer the live hand of the private entrepreneur to the dead hand of Socialism, but if the individual is to have social and industrial justice and to be guarded against what might become the tyranny of the strong, private enterprise must accept its duties, or even burdens. Its vigour and encouragement are indispensable in a progressive State, but it cannot operate law-free."

Robert Menzies, Inaugural Sir Robert Menzies Lecture, Perth, 12 May 1970

"Australian Liberals are not exponents of the 'open go', for if we are all to have an 'open go' – 'each for himself and the devil take the hindmost', anarchy will result and both security and progress will disappear."

Robert Menzies, Inaugural Sir Robert Menzies Lecture, Perth, 12 May 1970

"...though we are for the individual, we are too realistic to be egalitarian. We must leave levelling down to the Socialists. We believe passionately that in a civilised community every individual must be given his opportunity; that our educational provisions and our social and industrial laws should exist for his benefit; that he should be fitted and encouraged to develop the best he has in

him. But we cannot fail to know that although all men and women have equal political rights, and are regarded as equal in the eyes of the law, they are not and never will be equal to each other in talent, in vigour, or in character"

Robert Menzies, Inaugural Sir Robert Menzies Lecture, Perth, 12 May 1970

"Our individual citizen is to have self-discipline, to have duties as well as rights, to exist not as an isolated identity but as a civilised member of a civilised society which, expressing itself though a Parliament which it has freely chosen, makes laws which bind the individual. In that sense they limit his individual freedom and control many of his actions. But in the ultimate sense they guarantee his freedom against arbitrary interference, for discipline and freedom are not enemies but friends, so long as the discipline is, under a truly democratic system of government, socially self-imposed"

Robert Menzies, Inaugural Sir Robert Menzies Lecture, Perth, 12 May 1970

"Great enterprises seldom emerge by accident. They are much more frequently due to the work and inspiration of a man, of courage, imagination and determination"

Robert Menzies, Speech at the opening of the Emil Christensen Research Centre, Petersville [SA], 26 May 1971

"When we commenced the Liberal Party we had principles. Principles are apparently nowadays things that are not to be insisted upon because to insist upon them is to demonstrate that you are a 'reactionary' or 'a Conservative'. This, of course, is the most pernicious nonsense. Principles do not change. In the whole of my political life, I have never arrived at something that I thought to be a matter of principle lightly or casually. They have represented deep beliefs on my part; and I am old-fashioned enough to believe that principles, adopted after much thought and much consideration do not change. The circumstances to which they are to be applied, of course, will change with the change of circumstances, but the principles remain"

Robert Menzies, 'Looking Around at Eighty', Melbourne, 12 December 1974

"Liberalism has always stood for private enterprise, not an uncontrolled private enterprise, but a regulated private enterprise, because we have always believed that increased production is the best guarantee of economic stability, and that production is largely, if not wholly, to be achieved by private enterprise"

Robert Menzies, 'Looking Around at Eighty', Melbourne, 12 December 1974

12

Role of Government

The liberal philosophy of Menzies instinctively informed his view on the proper role and scope of government in civil society. Mindful of its capacities but also its limitations, government for Menzies always represented a means to an end and never an end in itself. There was much that a government could do to advance the wellbeing of its citizens, but it was profoundly unrealistic to expect it to provide the ultimate remedy to all of society's ills. Unlike the libertarian, Menzies did not regard government *per se* as an enemy of freedom but rejected the socialist view that the government itself represented the great source of freedom. In the British tradition of parliamentary democracy, Menzies saw government always as the servant of the people and never as their master. To invert this vital role of government, as the Nazi and Communist regimes had done in the twentieth century, would immediately open the door to dictatorship and the death of democracy. Accordingly, the destiny and fate of every government lay in the hands of the people who could elect it or dismiss it at will through the ballot box.

As well as being directly accountable to the people, Menzies saw the function of government as that of a machine, or utility instrument, to facilitate the peace, order and wellbeing of the country. He accepted that government had a legitimate role to raise taxes and distribute revenue, provide pensions and social security, organise defence, plan and execute public works such as the Snowy Mountains Hydro-electric Scheme, build infrastructure and public transport, provide education and health services, maintain civil order through the police and law enforcement agencies and to administer justice through the courts and judicial system. In addition, governments could also give leadership and direction to a society and promote a degree of cohesion amongst its citizens. For all these indispensable functions of government, however, Menzies emphasised that the source of human creativity, imagination and energy and enterprise could be found not in the government but in the people to whom it was accountable. It was individual men and women themselves who possessed the inspiration and enterprise to raise families, run businesses, build communities and care for the poor and disadvantaged. The supreme task of government, therefore, was to provide the ideal climate and opportunities for individuals to flourish spiritually, intellectually, socially and economically.

As to the citizens' attitude towards the role of government, Menzies was eager to remind his fellow Australians of their government's fiscal rights and responsibilities. The critical lesson Menzies was keen to impress on the people was that governments had no money of their own. Government could not be regarded as a free 'cash cow' from which citizens could derive entitlements for themselves, but rather as a treasury from which revenue was deposited from taxes to be then disbursed in public expenditure. The basic formula was that the sum of what all citizens received from the government could never exceed the sum of what all citizens contributed to the government in the first place. This was because the government, in itself, was no creator of wealth but rather an apparatus for the collection and distribution of existing national capital. For Menzies, the real creators and generators of wealth for the country were not governments but individuals and their free enterprises. The pathway to national prosperity therefore was not to increase government spending but to stimulate business growth and new employment opportunities for men and women to prosper.

With Menzies articulating his position on the role and scope of government, how did his own conception of government relate to that historically envisioned by liberalism? Given that Menzies envisaged a meaningful role for government in not only the fostering of private enterprise but also the amelioration of injustice, his creed of liberalism did differ from that of earlier figures such as Adam Smith and David Ricardo who preached *laissez-faire* economics. While obviously admiring the success of eighteenth-century classical liberalism in Britain for unleashing the enterprise and creativity of individuals, he was also mindful of its limitations. The classical liberals were right to stress that markets could accomplish things the state was incapable of doing, but were wrong to argue that the state could, and should, do nothing to alleviate the consequences of the market or interfere in the running of the workplace.[9] For Menzies, prudent state intervention, particularly in the form of humane labour laws and welfare provision, did not negate the liberal principles of free-enterprise and self-reliance. Rather, it was part of a balanced liberal programme that was both just and workable. For the liberal project to be fully realised, it was critical for individuals to pursue enterprise and self-sufficiency, but at the same time it was necessary for the state to ensure that the optimum economic and social conditions existed for individuals to take the initiative to work and thrive. The aim of state intervention, therefore, was to equip individuals with the wherewithal to succeed and not to give them a sense of welfare dependency and self-entitlement.

While Menzies' tradition of liberalism did allow for a moderate degree of state intervention, he was also mindful that assigning too great a role to government in society could imperil liberal principles. From his observation of State Socialism, he was aware that the existing rights for individuals to freely associate, speak, worship, assemble and partake in private enterprise could be impinged if the reach of government became too intrusive with policies such as bank nationalisation or compulsory unionism. As David Kemp appreciated, 'Menzies believed that Government had an important role, but it was limited in what it could achieve because its services and laws inevitably imposed conformity where progress required diversity'.

"I do not believe that we shall come out into the over-lordship of an all-powerful State on whose benevolence we shall live, spineless and effortless – a State which will dole out bread and ideas with neatly regulated accuracy; where we shall all have our dividend without subscribing our capital; where the Government, that almost deity, will nurse us and rear us and maintain us and pension us and bury us"

Robert Menzies, The Forgotten People Speech, 22 May 1942

"Individual enterprise must drive us forward. That does not mean that we are to return to the old and selfish notions of laissez-faire. The functions of the State will be much more than merely keeping the ring within which the competitors will fight. Our social and industrial obligations will be increased"

Robert Menzies, The Forgotten People Speech, 22 May 1942

"To every good citizen the State owes not only a chance in life but a self-respecting life. But this does not obscure the fact that the State cannot and must not put a premium on idleness or incompetence. It must still offer rewards to the enterprising."

Robert Menzies, Freedom from Want, 10 July 1942

"... there can be no real prosperity and happiness for all if we merely re-distribute the world's wealth without adding to it. In other words, a static material civilisation, with enterprise stifled by an iron-bound equality, with the dead hand of the State in control, will mean stagnation, and stagnation will ultimately mean a poverty which will be none the less real because it is shared by all"

Robert Menzies, Has Capitalism Failed? (Broadcast), 7 August 1942

"I am no believer in encouraging the notion that the citizen is simply dependent upon the State. It is a notion which is out of harmony with the tradition of the resourceful and independent Australian people. It is infinitely better that the State should be dependent upon the citizen."

Robert Menzies, Opening Speech, Camberwell Town Hall, 23 July 1943

"As citizens, we have for many years now in Australia developed an unrivalled technique in passing our responsibility on to other people, whether as in the particular when we say 'Why cannot he do it? He has more money than I have. He has more time than I have, and why cannot he do it?' – or in the general, 'Why does not the government do something about it?' As if the Government were some remote astral body indefinitely supplied and replenished with funds and able to do everything in Australia!"

Robert Menzies, The Christian Citizen in a New Era, St Columba Presbyterian Church, Woollahra, NSW, 27 February 1944

"The first task of government, therefore, is to restore what we call 'private business activity' instead of treating it, as Labour politicians frequently do, as if it were Public Enemy Number One. I ask you also to remember that employment on public works is in its very nature spasmodic; that it provides temporary jobs, and that it very seldom offers a real prospect of continuous employment, with progress and promotion"

Robert Menzies, Freemantle By-election, 15 August 1945

"We believe in the co-operation of Government and citizen, the Government formulating and enforcing social and industrial obligations, preserving true and fair competition by a strict control of all monopolistic tendency; co-operating with business in long range planning, while business itself supplies the drive and ambition and progress without which security will become a mere sham and living standards will fall, not rise. In a few words, Liberalism proposes to march down the middle of the road"

R. G. Menzies, Provisional Policy Statement, 31 August 1945

"A good Government...should treat private business as our good friend. There should be less nonsense talked about 'big business' as if private enterprise meant a few huge companies or control by a few men. If you add the individuals together, the greatest employers in Australia are the small businesses, the farmer, the small factory, the local shopkeeper"

Robert Menzies, "The Liberal Leader Speaks: Employment", Weekly Broadcast, 26 August 1949

"No government can give to any human being in this country any solitary thing that has not been sweated for and worked for by some other human being somewhere."

Robert Menzies, Speech at Wesley Church, Melbourne, 4 September 1949

"Governments do not exist merely to punish us for our errors, to threaten us with punishment in the future, to exercise rule over us whether it be harsh or gentle. Governments exist in a democracy first and foremost to give fire and character and direction to a country's thinking"

Robert Menzies, Speech at Wesley Church, Melbourne, 4 September 1949

"No Government could hope to solve it merely by giving way to special pressures within its own boundaries. The longer I live in public affairs the more satisfied I am that political leadership does not require the kind of mind which is blown about by every wind, but requires in full measure those very qualities of work and thought and determination and enterprise which we like to believe are the characteristic of the best elements in our nation and our people."

Robert Menzies, 'Australia Today – Man to Man', Broadcast, 16 September 1953

"It [the State] can organise defence better than you and I can. It can plan and carry out public works. It can devise and carry out the education of the young. It can keep the peace, and administer justice. But the dynamo, the driving force, of human progress is in the heart and mind and energy of the individual. Government is at best a machine."

Robert Menzies, 'Australia Today – Man to Man', Broadcast, 4 November 1953

"A community of individuals who expect and receive, at all stages of life, assistance and protection from the State must of necessity, by proper fiscal measures, accept the economic and financial burden of providing that assistance and protection. Many individuals may properly get from government more than they

pay to or provide for Government; some may even get "something for nothing" though I doubt it. But the sum of what all the individuals get cannot exceed the sum of what all the individuals pay or provide, for Government has no money of its own!"

Robert Menzies, Arthur E Mills Memorial Oration, Sydney, 11 May 1955

"If governments are to do more and more, let us at least see that they act in such a way as to preserve the greatest measure of independence of spirit, and do not sink into the error of creating a universal feeling of dependence upon government, or a willingness to accept as inevitable the complete regimentation of life by political authority"

Robert Menzies, Arthur E Mills Memorial Oration, Sydney, 11 May 1955

"This distinction between what Governments spend and set out to create and what private citizens spend and set out to create is not a clear cut distinction. There is a lot of overlapping here…because on analysis, you'll find that the great bulk of government investment on works provides the foundation upon which private enterprise can be established and expand. So we are not really enemies, we are not rivals in this field"

R. G. Menzies, Opening of De La Rue Factory, 14 March 1958

"Nothing that the Government of Victoria does, or that the Commission does, or that the Commonwealth does, ought to discourage individual effort, because Government Departments, with all the wisdom of their outlook which they occasionally achieve, cannot build into the bricks and mortar of a place like this, that spirit of kindliness which only individuals can produce"

Robert Menzies, Speech to open the Janet Biddlecombe wing of the Queen Elizabeth Home, 12 September 1959

"It is so easy to find a little money and think that we've done our duty to pay our taxes and say "Well, after all, I pay my taxes, let the Government look after it". I don't want somebody to say to me some day, nor to you, "Well we've paid our taxes, if you're in

trouble let the Government look after you". I would like to think that a few human beings were interested in me, wouldn't you?"

Robert Menzies, Speech to open the Janet Biddlecombe wing of the Queen Elizabeth Home, 12 September 1959

"What is the business of government? The business of government in the Commonwealth of Australia is to produce, to expound, to advocate great objectives of national policy. We are not here just to win an election. We are here to win something, to do something for our country. And therefore we must, at all times, try to behave according to the standards of statesmanship and not just according to the standards of vote-getting."

Robert Menzies, Young Liberals Rally, Hawthorn, 6 July 1962

"To compare the mechanism of government, as if it were some sentient creature with the genius of the human being is absurd"

Robert Menzies, Young Liberal Movement Convention, Sydney, 27 July 1962

"I don't believe that governments provide enterprise. I think governments may provide the condition in which enterprise is encouraged, but if you want enterprise, if you want vision, you have to go to the individual human being. It is human beings right through the community who do things, who think out things, who get on with them"

Robert Menzies, Young Liberal Movement Convention, Sydney, 27 July 1962

"What governments can and should do, when encountering some new problem or developing state of affairs, is not to say "the Government will run this", but first of all to seek the private enterprise answer, to help the individual to help himself, to create, by legislation and administration, a social economic and industrial climate favourable to his activity and growth"

Robert Menzies, First Baillieu Lecture, 6 July 1964

"Governments do not create wealth, though frequently they will

distribute it for the public benefit. Governments, contrary to a well-known political superstition, have no money of their own. In the field of public finance, they spend what men and women have earned and have paid to them in either taxes or loans"

Robert Menzies, 'The Science and Art of Politics', University of Texas Lectures (No 1), 20 November 1969

"The greatest function of a democratic government is to create a climate in which enterprise will flourish and productivity will increase, in which not only will human physical progress develop, but the human mind expand and the human spirit constantly revive"

Robert Menzies, 'The Science and Art of Politics', University of Texas Lectures (No 1), 20 November 1969

"We recognise that the State has great functions to perform which are far beyond the scope of private enterprise. The ancient idea that government's only function was to 'keep the ring' while the private enterprise contestants slogged it out has no place in our Liberal philosophy. On the contrary, we recognise that the State has very wide responsibilities; by appropriate economic and monetary measures to assist in preventing large-scale unemployment; by social and industrial legislation to provide a high degree of economic security and justice for all its citizens. It must have progressive housing policies, accept great responsibilities in such disparate matters as education and transportation, ports and railways"

Robert Menzies, Inaugural Sir Robert Menzies Lecture, Perth, 12 May 1970

"Governments have their part to play. They may regulate, they may distribute, but they do not create, and, therefore, what happens to private enterprise is of vital importance to the people of Australia"

Robert Menzies, 'Looking Around at Eighty', Melbourne, 12 December 1974

13

Liberty and Democracy

At the heart of Menzies' liberal philosophy was his unshakable faith in the essential goodness of democracy. As a young man in 1917, he asserted that the social fabric of a society must be based on democratic values, not least the 'rights and liberties of the individual'. As Menzies entered political and public life, his faith in democracy only strengthened as he recognised this as the edifice by which the modern civilisations of Britain, Australia and the West were sustained. In the philosophical tradition of John Locke and the Founders of the United States, the essential element to a democracy was the existence of the 'social contract', an unwritten convention that bound the citizens of a society together by a set of mutual rights and obligations. If the citizens of such a society, however, insisted only on their rights and ignored their obligations, then the contract would be breached and democracy would suffer. Accordingly, the model democrat was the citizen who always viewed their own rights in relation to the competing rights of their fellow citizens. In Menzies own words, 'we must be givers rather than receivers; we must be quick to discharge our duties and modest about our rights'. The survival of a democratic state thereby depended, to a large degree, on the unselfish spirit of its own citizens and their quest to seek the wellbeing of their neighbour and the common good of the polity.

The great genius of modern democracy, according to Menzies, was its demonstrated capacity to withstand human fallibility. Far from promising a perfect society, democracy lent itself to a process of 'trial and error' that allowed public opinion to be continually tested, moulded and refined in a society's mission to advance the wellbeing of its people. Through a citizenry's experience of participatory democracy with their personal rights to decide, to elect, to reject, to debate and to criticise, they would acquire the wisdom to arrive at a correct position on a given issue, even where they may have been wrong previously. The flexibility and responsiveness of democracy allowed for previous errors of judgment in public opinion or policy to be seamlessly rectified with minimal disruption to the body-politic. Recognising that the human judgment of any given leader could by no means be invariably infallible, democracy provided the forum for such judgments to be rigorously scrutinised, debated and held to account by both the legislature and the broader electorate. For Menzies, it was this realist essence of democracy that distinguished it from the alternatives of Fascism, Nazism and Communism with their utopian boast of human perfectibility.

As anti-democratic statist ideologies, Menzies saw Fascism, Nazism and Communism as inimical to the interest of the people. Instead of existing as free people with inherent dignity and rights, the people in such regimes became slaves to a merciless, all-powerful state. In contrast to the governments of democratic societies which focused first and foremost on procuring the domestic wellbeing of their people, the governments of anti-democratic regimes were preoccupied simply with amassing their own power and prestige. This was of course anathema to the English tradition that the state operated as the *servant* of the people, a notion rooted in both Christianity and the Enlightenment. For Menzies, it was impossible for democracy to exist unless the people were the masters with the government dependent on the people. The people were the masters in the sense that government had no authority and no privilege beyond that granted by the people themselves. This democratic principle explained why Australia's constitutional founders had drafted the nation's supreme body of law in such a way that it could only be altered by the assent of the people in a referendum.

The other defining feature of democracy for Menzies was that it represented not so much a machine but a 'spirit'. To be sure, modern democracy relied upon the legislative, executive and judicial machinery of government for its operation but its essence and inspiration was a spirit. According to Menzies, it was a spirit drawn from the Christian belief that human beings bore the image of God and stood equal in the eyes of their creator. Like the drafters of the American Declaration of Independence, Menzies believed that this afforded every individual citizen the right to life, liberty and the pursuit of happiness, the very rights deemed essential to the spirit of democracy. As a spirit, therefore, democracy functioned as a driving force for social progress to elevate the dignity of men and women, to build up moral character, to advance peace and to realise justice and fairness for all. As such, it resembled a perennial force of civilisation rather than just another system of government that waxed and waned in the procession of human history.

For Menzies, the freedom-loving ideals of democracy and liberalism were complementary, essentially serving the same purpose of social progress. While leaders of free nations have frequently assumed democracy to be simply a 'given', all too often taken for granted, Menzies appreciated the genius of its historical evolution over centuries. Remarking that 'we have been too close to democracy to appreciate it', he gave special attention to publicly outline its achievements of peace, freedom, superior living standards, technological advancement, humane social reform and class cooperation in the accomplishment of the democratic project. Owing to the fact that the development of authentic democracy was historically *gradual*, Menzies held that it was unwise and naïve for otherwise well-meaning Western democracies to expect their own system of government to be successfully transplanted to places where liberal principles were non-existent. Just as an uprooted crop would have difficulty flourishing in alien soil, a democracy would encounter great trouble taking root in civilisations where natural rights and the individual freedoms of expression, association, religion, assembly, trade and commerce were still foreign concepts. Like the historical experience of Britain over centuries, the people of a society would first of all need to be schooled in these precepts before it could develop the institutions of parliamentary democracy for itself. As Menzies was fond of reminding his audience, the spirit of liberty and democracy derived not from institutions and statutes but from the hearts of ordinary men and women.

"It has long since been recognised that if all men are to be equal before the law, then the social fabric must be based on as full a recognition as possible of the rights and liberties of the individual"

Robert Menzies, 'The Rule of Law during the War', Bowen Prize Essay, University of Melbourne, 1917

"All things considered we have probably made our greatest advances in the realm of bodily freedom. Most of our current materialist political philosophy has been directed to the attainment of a higher degree of bodily well-being…But the conception of a liberated body inhabited by a stunted mind and a poor spirit is not a noble one. It is, therefore, to the problem of mental and spiritual freedom that we must turn if we are to assess accurately the place that freedom is taking in our modern civilisation"

Robert Menzies, Freedom in Modern Society, 1935

"We are accustomed to the phenomenon of the trade cycle; let us also remember that there are other cycles, and that one of them, readily enough discernible in modern European history, is the cycle by which liberty degenerates into license, license produces its inevitable reaction, and reaction re-establishes the rigours of authority"

Robert Menzies, Freedom in Modern Society, 1935

"Here, indeed, is the final, though paradoxical truth; that although the essence of democracy is that the majority shall rule, democracy can never be the real instrument of freedom unless its majorities are constantly contending for the rights of their minorities"

Robert Menzies, Freedom in Modern Society, 1935

"The picture of our Elysium is not of a place where freedom is to the strong, but of a place where freedom is to the weak; where the majority will rule, but will insist upon the minority's right to disagree with them; where the humblest citizen will punctually

and indeed reverently obey the law because, though it may be a poor thing, it is his own"

Robert Menzies, Freedom in Modern Society, 1935

"In a word, a good democracy wants good democrats; and the good democrat is not the man who prates loudly of his rights and thinks of government in terms of individual or class interests, but the man who realises that the social contract which binds any society together is one expressed primarily in terms of duties and of obligations"

Robert Menzies, 'Is Democracy Doomed', Broadcast Address for ABC, 1935-36

"The great quality of democracy is that it is flexible and responsive to changed opinion, and lends itself readily to that process of trial and error by which progress comes and the truth prevails. Thus, it is that though the majority may be wrong today, that courage and patience on the part of those actively engaged in affairs, with wisdom which is born of bitter experience, will make the majority right tomorrow"

Robert Menzies, 'Is Democracy Doomed', Broadcast Address for ABC, 1935-36

"Democracy demands leaders and leadership. It demands leaders who will not be afraid to tell the people that they are wrong and to persuade and guide them. I do not deny, on the contrary I uphold, the right of the people to censure freely, to criticise, to elect, to reject"

Robert Menzies, The Place of a University in a Modern Community, p 30, 1939

"The great vice of democracy is that for a generation we have been busy getting ourselves on to the list of beneficiaries and removing ourselves from the list of contributors, as if somewhere there was somebody else's effort on which we could thrive."

Robert Menzies, The Forgotten People Speech, 22 May 1942

"Here we touch upon one of the great maladies of democracy, a malady which can easily become malignant and destroy us; that rather futile and supine acceptance of the idle and false doctrine that the Government owes us everything while we owe the government nothing"

Robert Menzies, The Government and Ourselves, Broadcast 3AW, 5 June 1942

"Any visitor from another planet, making an examination of the character and habits of our people, and searching for the main-spring of that love of freedom which distinguishes us, would find it not in Acts of Parliament or blue books or dusty records, but in the hearts of the people themselves"

Robert Menzies, Constitutional Guarantees, Broadcast 3AW, 27 November 1942

"A free Press must not set itself up to be the masters of the people, for in a democratic community the people should prefer the master they have themselves chosen to those who are merely self-appointed. In other words, a free Press must not seek to maintain its freedom at the expense of popular freedom and popular self-government"

Robert Menzies, Freedom of Speech and Expression, 26 June 1942

"Freedom of association is of the first order of importance in the world of liberty. It is important that I should be free to associate with other people who think as I do. It is not always realised that it is equally important that I should be free not to associate with people who do not think as I do"

Robert Menzies, Compulsory Unionism, 11 August 1942

"Democracy, being founded upon the rights of the individual citizens, concerns itself first and foremost with the domestic well-being of its people. It occupies itself with political and social and industrial reform"

Robert Menzies, The Achievements of Democracy, 6 November 1942

"Democracy is more than a machine; it is a spirit. It is based upon the Christian conception that there is in every human soul a spark of the divine; that, with all their inequalities of mind and body, the souls of men stand equal in the sight of God. So it is that, while Fascists and Nazis concentrate their efforts upon the power of the State, regarding the citizen as the mere minister to that power, democrats must concern themselves with what they see to be the true end and final justification of the State – a full and good life for every individual citizen"

Robert Menzies, The Nature of Democracy, 23 October 1942

"... if we are to live together in mutual amity and justice, if we are to be dignified without being proud or overbearing, we must be givers rather than receivers; we must be quick to discharge our duties and modest about our rights"

Robert Menzies, The Nature of Democracy, 23 October 1942

"What, then, must democracy do if it is to be a real force in the new world? In my opinion, two things. It must recapture the vision of the good man as the purpose of government. And it must restore the authority and prestige of Parliament as the supreme organic expression of self-governement"

Robert Menzies, The Task of Democracy, 13 November 1942

"To develop every human being to his fullest capacity for thought, for action, for sacrifice and for endurance is our major task"

Robert Menzies, The Task of Democracy, 13 November 1942

"Among my theories is a firm belief that no democracy can survive as a democracy if its Parliament becomes a mere rudderless ship, without chart or sailing directions, without order, with a crew of independents whose prime qualification for enlistment was their ignorance of navigation and their contempt for discipline"

Robert Menzies, The Party System, Broadcast, 15 January 1943

"Democracy cannot succeed merely by grace of a few leaders or a few thinkers. It must develop its citizens to the limit of their individual intelligence. It can never rest on its laurels while any boy or girl

lacks the opportunity to become a trained and qualified citizen"

Robert Menzies, Opening Speech, Camberwell Town Hall, 23 July 1943

"To the Liberal Democrat, therefore, one of the first tests to be applied to any scheme of social betterment is whether it pauperises the individual by making him dependent upon community charity or whether it elevates and dignifies the individual by giving him his social benefits as a matter of right, and as a result of it, among other things, his own efforts"

Robert Menzies, Social Security, Broadcast, 17 September 1943

"I have a deep-seated conviction that with all its faults the true strength of democracy lies in its elevation of the ordinary man and its recognition of the fact that there are amazing possibilities in every boy and girl. If we are to develop these possibilities, if we are to match with proper care our rights and our duties as citizens, surely there can be no doubt that every measure of reform we take must have in mind, as Sir William Beveridge said – 'that the State in organising security should not stifle incentive, opportunity, responsibility"

R. G. Menzies, Social Security, Broadcast, 17 September 1943

"The choice in practical terms is between Communism or Fascism on the one hand, and an enlightened Liberal system on the other, which has no desire whatever to go back to unrestricted and ruthless competition, but which does see in the system of individual initiative a driving quality, a motive power, an instrument of progress which is of such great value to mankind that to destroy it would be to inflict almost untold hardships upon future generations"

R. G. Menzies, A Liberal Revival, Broadcast, 29 October 1943

"Why should people worry about whether the majority vote is against them? We should be much better employed in the new order by worrying as to whether we are right, because, if we believe that we are right, then some day that which we stand for will win."

Robert Menzies, The Christian Citizen in a New Era,

St Columba Presbyterian Church, Woollahra, NSW, 27 February 1944

"Democrats cannot be either Fascist or Communist. They abhor dictatorship, whether it is built on the German model or on the Russian one. They suspect...that as practical systems of Government, their controlled unions, their abolition of really representative Parliaments, their secret police, their suppression of individual freedom, have far more in common with each other than either of them has with Parliamentary Democracy"

Robert Menzies, 'What is Australian Communism?', Broadcast, 1946

"We need constantly to remind ourselves that democracy can produce tyranny just as readily as any other system of government unless the individual democrat has learned to attach supreme importance to individual freedom"

Robert Menzies, The Choice, Broadcast, 1946

"There is another freedom which is under challenge today, and this is a very important freedom, because without it our immortal souls will be in deadly peril. It is the freedom to do our best to make that best better. This is a great freedom"

Robert Menzies, 'Bond or Free', Wesley Church, Melbourne, 7 September 1947

"If freedom means only full stomachs and comfortable beds, then there are millions of slaves who enjoy freedom"

Robert Menzies, 'Bond or Free', Wesley Church, Melbourne, 7 September 1947

"If freedom connotes the full use of the powers that God has given man, then there can be no freedom in the all-powerful State or in the servile mass mind which Smuts described as the greatest menace of our time"

Robert Menzies, 'Bond or Free', Wesley Church, Melbourne, 7 September 1947

"Democracy rests upon the view that the people are the rulers as well as the ruled; that the government has no authority and no privilege beyond that granted by the people themselves; that while sovereignty attaches to the acts of the parliament, that sovereignty is derived from the people and has no other source"

Robert Menzies, The Banking Bill (1947), Second Reading Speech, House of Representatives, 23 October 1947

"The whole history of democracy which, we should be proud to say, is still primarily the history of the English speaking peoples, is one of struggle for the control of government by the people, not for control of people by the government – for that freedom which can exist only when the powers of government are limited, when legislators and administrators are responsible to the people, and when no great changes in the material structure of life can be made without popular mandate and approval"

Robert Menzies, The Banking Bill (1947), Second Reading Speech, House of Representatives, 23 October 1947

"The odd thing about democracy, the thing that distinguishes it from every other form of human government that has been tried, is that in a democracy the rulers and the ruled are the same people. The same people have the powers and the responsibilities. The same people have the rights and the duties"

Robert Menzies, Speech at Wesley Church, Melbourne, 4 September 1949

"It is the difficult but profound truth about democracy that each one of us must learn to be both ruler and subject, both the law-maker and obeyer of the law."

Robert Menzies, Speech at Wesley Church, Melbourne, 4 September 1949

"You see, the oldest expression of democracy – a word which you cannot find in the New Testament – is inherent in the question 'am I my brother's keeper?'"

Robert Menzies, Speech at Wesley Church, Melbourne, 4 September 1949

"There is no democracy except where the people are the masters, where government is dependent on the people and where the people are not dependent on the Government."

Robert Menzies, Speech at Wesley Church, Melbourne, 4 September 1949

"Democracy cannot be and must not be a sterile or selfish thing if it is to succeed. Democracy must demand from all of us all our skill, all our unselfishness, all our honest independence of mind."

Robert Menzies, Speech at Wesley Church, Melbourne, 4 September 1949

"If democracy is to be a mere levelling down it will bring with it lower standards and a less noble conception of life. It must be a levelling up, a constant struggle for the highest, an unceasing encouragement to all of us to do our best, to develop our character and skill and energy."

Robert Menzies, Speech at Wesley Church, Melbourne, 4 September 1949

"The character of democracy does not depend upon its laws, it depends upon the character of its individual men and women. In a true democracy the State does not and cannot make the people. It is the people who make the State."

Robert Menzies, Speech at Wesley Church, Melbourne, 4 September 1949

"Democracy is neither accidental nor inevitable. It is the product of generations of self-sacrifice, of conscious struggle, of belief in the vital significance of individual men and women, of a sense of a Divine order in a distracted human world"

Robert Menzies, Broadcast on the Occasion of Australia's Jubilee Celebrations, 9 May 1951

"In a democracy, the Government is ourselves, and nobody else"

Robert Menzies, 'Australia Today – Man to Man', Broadcast, 4 November 1953

"If we are all tired democrats, eager beneficiaries but reluctant contributors, democracy would collapse under its own weight"

Robert Menzies, The First William Queale Memorial Lecture, Adelaide, 22 October 1954

"For democracy's true glory is not the achievement of a uniform mediocrity or of a spirit of dependence upon government, but the encouragement of talent and initiative, the elevation of the individual, the giving of opportunity to all who have the inherent quality to seize it"

Robert Menzies, The First William Queale Memorial Lecture, Adelaide, 22 October 1954

"What we are defending in our various countries and under our various agreements is not some man, not some government, but the freedom of the people of that country. If they are to change their government they must be allowed to change it in their own way. If they are to adopt new philosophies, they must adopt them in their own way. But we are not going to accept a position in which, by force from without, these people are converted into being the slaves of some new tyranny"

Robert Menzies, Address to the United States Congress, 15 March 1955

"The glory of democratic self-government is that it has not only lifted the status and expanded the horizons of ordinary men and women, but has also produced some of the greatest and wisest and bravest men of modern times. It is only by remembering this and rejoicing in it that we can hope to escape the deadly cynicism about politics which, with its clammy hand, reduces enthusiasms and discourages generous effort"

Robert Menzies, Address to the Royal Australasian College of Physicians, Sydney, 11 May 1955

"Being a democrat just doesn't consist of going along to vote once in however many years it may be, doesn't consist of having violent opinions about one politician or another, [it] doesn't consist of going along to some political meeting and demanding something for me as so many people will. The task of democracy is to understand

what is good for the whole of the people"

Robert Menzies, Speech at Wesley Church, Melbourne, 4 September 1955

"The task of a good democrat is frequently to abandon his own claims in favour of the claims of others. Indeed at its best it is the task of a good democrat to be prepared to vote to injure his own interests if he thinks what he is voting for is good for the community"

Robert Menzies, Speech at Wesley Church, Melbourne, 4 September 1955

"Every democrat has the task of contributing his or her thought to the government of the country…Don't let's delegate our thinking to a few, because when we delegate our thinking to a few we correspondingly delegate power to a few"

Robert Menzies, Speech at Wesley Church, Melbourne, 4 September 1955

"Where men are equal before the law, where the writ runs without fear or favour or affection, where parliament sits, without threat, to represent the people of the country, there you have the very definition of liberty"

Robert Menzies, Address to the Joint Session of the Congress of the Philippines, 23 April 1957

"Democracy is a business in which you must get from every individual the best that he has in him and get him to understand that he is not just engaged in a purely individual effort but is part of a community enterprise so that he must have a sense of community. He must have a firm mind, he must have a clear character but he must know that there are interests other than his own. That is the very essence of democracy"

R. G. Menzies, Management and the Future of Australia, 1957

"I invite you to remember with pride that it was in the free world that the two great institutions of liberty, Parliamentary self-government and the rule of honestly administered law, were fashioned"

Robert Menzies, Address to the Tenth Session of the Australasian Medical Congress, Hobart, 5 March 1958

"From the point of view of democracy it is much better for a man to be out by exercising his own mind and character than to be in by abandoning them"

Robert Menzies, Speech at St Mark's Library Canberra, 27 August 1959

"The great tasks of democracy are...to achieve peace, to achieve goodwill, to develop individual freedom, to prefer the interests of ordinary men and women, to put the search for the truth at the top of the list, to encourage straight living and straight talking"

Robert Menzies, National Press Club Luncheon, Washington, 25 May 1959

"Do you suppose that you can take a community of many millions of people, not bred in our tradition, not with that fusion that has gone on for so many centuries with us, between the principles of Christianity and the principles of representative Government, bred in some strange creed, from our point of view, with notable cultures going back into their own history, but incapable of being understood by us, or by many of us, at any rate. You can't take a fully grown plant, like our parliamentary democracy, and put it down in an alien soil and expect it to flourish and grow and bear its fruit as if it had been there all its life"

Robert Menzies, Speech to Central Methodist Mission, 6 September 1959

"The great free powers are on trial today: none more so than the greatest of them, the United States of America. The way in which they survive this trial will depend upon how they rise to the splendid, but awful responsibility of power: how bravely they guard the inner liberties of man: how utterly they cast out fear; how clearly their light shines before men; how far they keep the feeling of adventure, and avoid the defensiveness of riches"

Robert Menzies, Speech at Harvard University, 16 June 1960

"Don't let us fall into the error of thinking that by waving a wand, a Communist dictator can strike out of the hearts and minds of people their passion for freedom. They may control them with their

beliefs; they may control them with threats and commands. But freedom is not such a fragile plant. Freedom dies hard. And there are millions of people in Europe today whose passion for freedom is not destroyed by the presence of a Communist Commissar"

Robert Menzies, Second Freedom Rally, Melbourne, 5 November 1960

"The truth is that the great glory of democracy is that it does pay attention to the individual person. The authoritarian systems that exist in other countries tend to reduce the individual to a mere cipher, to a mere calculating medium in a blue book, or a statistical record. But in democracy it is the man and the woman who count. The business of Government is to promote them, to enlarge their opportunities, to broaden their horizons, to develop their personalities"

Robert Menzies, Citizens Luncheon, Ashfield Town Hall, 15 May 1961

"I detect in our own democracy a weakness, it is simply that I think that occasionally…we think too much of our rights, and too little of our responsibilities. Because if we think of our rights only, of our demands only, of our claims on Government only, then we will transfer the responsibility for meeting those claims to a smaller and smaller body of men; until ultimately, we'll find that we have brought about a system of oligarchy or bureaucracy, or even of autocracy, because the responsibility has been piled on to other people while we ourselves assert our rights"

Robert Menzies, Citizens Luncheon, Ashfield Town Hall, 15 May 1961

"For the greatest of all liberties is that which exists in a man's own mind. It is a liberty of which he alone is master, and it makes him to that extent a master, not a servant. Produce in a nation a generation of men and women with liberty in their own individual minds, and dictatorship becomes impossible"

Robert Menzies, The Challenge to Education, 19 May 1961

"Free communities can provide for their citizens growing living standards and swift national development without the sacrifice of individual freedom in the interests of a dictatorship or a powerful few"

Robert Menzies, Luncheon in Honour of Japan PM, Canberra, 30 January 1963

"You cannot endow a country with democracy as simply as you can endow it with money or goods"

Robert Menzies, The Battle for Freedom, Jefferson Oration, Charlottesville, Virginia, 4 July 1963

"Democracy can't be built from the top down. Democracy has to be built from the bottom up, and the reason why so many of these new countries have become, in reality, dictatorships with no parliamentary oppositions with no opponents worth talking about to the powers-that-be, the reason is that these countries started at the wrong end"

R. G. Menzies, Civic Reception, Albany (WA), 11 October 1964

"Freedom, in my opinion, is one of the great innate attributes of human nature and it's therefore universal in its inner aspects. It's not divisible you can't sell out on the freedom of one country and think that you have protected the freedom of your own"

Robert Menzies, Address to the American Australian Association, New York, 11 June 1965

"It is this divine right of men to live free from aggression, free from unprovoked violence living in their own homes in their own country without fear of attack, which is one of the great human rights"

Robert Menzies, American-Australian Association Luncheon, New York, 11 June 1965

"True democracy seeks to achieve not justice to a few or something for the talented but justice for all men, for all women, and regards the good life of the individual as the ultimate aim of government"

Robert Menzies, Hoskins Family Memorial Service at Hoskins Memorial Church, Lithgow [NSW], 17 October 1965

"No act of Parliament can make a nation prosperous. No set of regulations can get rid of human error, or, of its own force, create prosperity. For, in a democracy, it is the energetic citizen who produces wealth, and the idler, the non-contributor, who impairs the efficiency of the process"

Robert Menzies, 'The Science and Art of Politics', University of Texas Lectures (No 1), 20 November 1969

"The glory of democracy is an intelligent and educated community"

Robert Menzies, 'The Science and Art of Politics', University of Texas Lectures (No 1), 20 November 1969

14

Monarchy and Crown

The Crown and monarchy eminently appealed to both the British and democratic instincts of Menzies. For Menzies, the Crown represented the great fountainhead of British institutions and traditions including the Established Churches of England and Scotland, the judiciary and the English Common Law, the executive arms of government, the Privy Council and the whole Westminster system of Parliamentary democracy. Through the British Empire and then the Commonwealth, the Crown also provided a global network between different countries around the world which shared a common British heritage. Although many such countries eventually became republics they still honoured the British monarch as head of the Commonwealth. To affirm the supreme status of the Crown in Australia meanwhile, the Menzies government enacted the *Royal Style and Titles Act* (1953) which declared Her Majesty to be 'Elizabeth the Second, by the grace of God, of the United Kingdom, Australia and her other Realms and Territories Queen, Head of the Commonwealth, Defender of the Faith'.

Despite originating from a pre-democratic age, the ever-adaptable monarchy was esteemed by Menzies as the great bulwark of modern democracy. As an impartial umpire detached from the cut and thrust of partisan politics, a modern constitutional monarchy provided the necessary space for a robust democracy to thrive and flourish without undue interference. The fact that the monarchy was able to survive Britain's gradual evolution to a mature democracy since the 1688 Glorious Revolution was testament to its adjustability to the modern age. In Britain's historical journey from an absolute to a constitutional monarchy, Menzies observed that 'as the powers of the people, through Parliament, have come to be paramount, so have the powers of the Crown diminished'. Even from developments in his own lifetime, Menzies remarked on how King George V 'accommodated himself to the new democracy and the new Commonwealth' of the interwar years as the 1931 Statute of Westminster established legislative equality for the self-governing dominions of the British Empire.

The attachment of Menzies to the Crown and monarchy was not only formal and professional but also deeply personal, a fact brought home when Queen Elizabeth personally bestowed an Order of Australia on a wheelchair-bound Menzies at the Melbourne Cricket Ground in March 1977. Born in the twilight of Queen Victoria's reign and growing up in the reign of Edward VII, his public career in State and Federal politics spanned the reign of four more monarchs including George V, Edward VIII, George VI and Elizabeth II. He was perhaps the only Prime Minister of Australia, and only one of the few in the Empire/Commonwealth, to enjoy a close relationship with the Royal family which dated from his first visit to London in 1935, for King George V's jubilee celebrations, and lasted until the silver jubilee celebrations of Elizabeth II in 1977. One of the high points in Menzies' personal relationship with the monarchy was the warm rapport he enjoyed with King George VI and his wife, Queen Elizabeth, during the tumultuous years of World War II. At first hand, he appreciated the encouragement the King and Queen gave to the ordinary people of Britain with their comforting presence in the besieged streets of London. Paying tribute to George VI in February 1952, Menzies told parliament that the departed King had brought the Crown 'closer to the people' and in the bitter crisis of war, 'served us all so well [as] ruler, and leader, and friend'.

By hosting regular royal visits to Australia, Menzies was able to not only continue his warm personal relations with the monarchy but endear the Crown to the Australian public. Under the post-war Menzies government, royal visits became more frequent than before the war and this helped make the monarchy more personal and less distant to ordinary Australians. Accompanied by her husband the Duke of Edinburgh, Queen Elizabeth II became the first reigning monarch to visit Australian shores in early 1954. Touring the country for two months, she was seen by an estimated three in four Australians. Royal visits by the Duke of Edinburgh followed in 1956 and 1965, and Queen Elizabeth the Queen Mother in 1958. The Queen herself visited Australia once more during Menzies' Prime Ministership in 1963 where she made the Prime Minister a Knight of the Thistle. Menzies enjoyed these occasions immensely but was conscious of not 'overdoing' royal visits for fear of provoking boredom or cynicism amongst the Australian public.

Following his retirement from office in 1966, Menzies' support for the Crown and monarchy remained steadfast. Representing 'this history of centuries', the Crown for Menzies remained a 'focal point, a centre of gravity, without which no nation can survive'. In constitutional monarchies such as Australia, the Queen was seen as 'the fountain of honour, the protector of the law and the centre of a Parliamentary system'. Not surprisingly, Menzies was sceptical about the merits of Australia becoming a republic and remained unconvinced by the arguments advanced by Australian republicans in the late 1960s. He maintained that the apolitical office of the Crown gave it a natural superiority over both executive and non-executive presidencies where periodic elections would serve invariably to politicise the office of President. He also questioned the claims of republicans that a president would be necessarily 'closer to the people' than a monarch, with the office of presidency merely substituting one form of pomp and officialdom for another. While Menzies acknowledged the success of the American republic, he appreciated the unique historical context in which it had emerged. The republic of the United States was the product of a popular Revolution against an autocratic monarch, whereas Australia on the other hand had 'inherited a system of Responsible Government and then a Constitutional Monarchy in the true sense'. With the advantage of these nineteenth and twentieth century developments, Menzies did not see Australian democracy as standing to benefit from any future transition to a republic.

"The Crown is, in the whole of our British world, our symbol of unity. It is more than that. It is the focal point of a deep and moving loyalty and love. It gives structure to the British Commonwealth"

Robert Menzies, Speech to the Senate, 7 February 1952

"To our new Queen, Elizabeth the Second, so young, so full of loveliness and grace and character, and so informed by tradition and training, we should all like to say words of comfort and encouragement...As she goes through her sorrow to her great responsibilities it would be the wish of all of us to say to her that we have faith in her; that we are her sworn counsellors in this portion of her realm, sworn willingly both in hand and in heart; and that, with God's help, we are resolved to do all that we may to make her reign as rich and kind and good and memorable as that of her illustrious father"

Robert Menzies, Speech to the Senate, 7 February 1952

"The Crown serves as the legal nexus between all the British countries and all the British people; that, because it is the legal nexus, the existence of the Crown converts what would otherwise be a friendly partnership of people with some common interests into a structure, into something organic, into something which rises far superior to a partnership of convenience"

Robert Menzies, "The British Crown", Speech at the Constitutional Association of New South Wales, Sydney, 9 October 1953

"The Governor-General is The Queen's personal representative in this country, and therefore, through her Governor-General, the Queen is present in Canberra at the opening of Parliament, just as she is present at the opening of Parliament in Cape Town, Ottawa, Wellington, or wherever it may be around the British Commonwealth"

Robert Menzies, "The British Crown", Speech at the Constitutional Association of New South Wales, Sydney, 9 October 1953

"It is one of those strokes of genius that have come about throughout the history of our race. We still have a Crown, once regarded as the

enemy of democracy, and we have that Crown as the central feature of democracy, as its highest instrument for self-government"

Robert Menzies, "The British Crown", Speech at the Constitutional Association of New South Wales, Sydney, 9 October 1953

"First, the Queen represents free self-government. She is, by the very words of the Australian Constitution, part of the Australian Parliament. As such, she makes our Acts of Parliament 'by and with the advice and consent of the Senate and the House of Representatives', and in no other way. Here existence on the Throne is therefore not a mark of tyranny, but a guarantee of Parliamentary freedom"

Robert Menzies, 'Australia Today – Man to Man', Broadcast, 10 March 1954

"I have no doubt that those who write the British constitutional history of the 20th century will be struck by the fact that George V and George VI had the task more than their predecessors, of first reconciling the position of the Crown with the strong democratic developments of their time and then adapting it to the new concept of the Commonwealth of free and equal nations"

Robert Menzies, 'Australia Today – Man to Man', Broadcast, 12 March 1958

"This genius for monarchy has not disappeared, indeed the more I think about it, the more I believe that in our own time, our own Royal Family has managed magnificently to combine the place and dignity of the throne with the ordinary life, the ordinary desires and needs of ordinary human beings"

Robert Menzies, Speech at 50th Anniversary of the Founding of Canberra, 25 November 1960

"There are clever people in the world - at least so I understand - who have discovered that all sorts of things ought to be done to the Monarchy to democratise the Monarchy, to do something to it, to do something to what we all are proud to say is the most democratic Monarchy in the whole wide world"

Robert Menzies, Reception at Parliament House in Honour

of Her Majesty the Queen, 18 February 1963

"I am a monarchist just because to me, and millions of others, the Crown is non-utilitarian; it represents a spiritual and emotional conception more enduring and significant than any balance sheet cast up by an accountant"

Robert Menzies, Afternoon Light, 1967, p 234

"For I am an unrepentant monarchist; I believe in the significance of the Crown in our British system of Government; and above all I believe that in my time we have had monarchs of high character and powerful personality, who have made a notable contribution to our history, who have been real contributors to the continuity of our institutions, and whose status, both official and personal, has helped to establish that simple sense of continuity and endurance to which the world has owed so much in two great wars"

Robert Menzies, Afternoon Light, 1967, p 238

"The present Queen, who is the most remarkable monarch since the first Elizabeth, has done so much to strengthen the position of the Crown and to inspire general respect for it that I am constantly horrified to find that some alleged intellectuals in Australia want to have a Republic. I hope they fail most dismally. I am proud to name myself a loyal servant of the Queen"

Robert Menzies, Message for the British Society, Melbourne, 19 January 1977

"The greatest system of political government yet devised is that of responsible government under the Crown"

Robert Menzies, Message for the British Society, Melbourne, 19 January 1977

15

Parliament and Politics

From his election to the Victorian Legislative Council in 1928 to his retirement from the House of Representatives in 1966, parliament represented the central forum to Menzies' public life. Menzies served in two parliaments, the Victorian and the Commonwealth; and three chambers, the Legislative Council and Legislative Assembly of Victoria followed by the House of Representatives in Canberra. With his penchant for oratory, repartee and persuasive advocacy honed by years of practice at the bar, Menzies is widely credited for mastering the medium of parliament. For Menzies, parliament served not only a mechanical function as a law-making body but as a public platform for national leaders to articulate their political philosophy and to propound their vision for the nation to the people. As the theatre of representative democracy, the parliament provided the forum for ideas and policies always to be scrutinised, debated and tested on their merits. As such it acted as a vital check on the despotic impulses of government by keeping it accountable to its political masters, the electors of Australia. Whilst no doubt encountering all the normal frustrations of obstruction, delay and division associated with parliamentary proceedings, Menzies regarded the institution of parliament as indispensable to 'ordered liberty'.

Given his high esteem for parliament, he maintained the greatest reverence for its Westminster conventions and deplored any conduct that brought the institution into disrepute. With Menzies appreciating the

Australian people's ownership of parliament, breaches of parliamentary decorum by its members served only to treat the public with contempt. Critical to maintaining the good name of parliament was, of course, the personal conduct of individual parliamentarians. For Menzies, a good parliament could only exist with good members and this meant that the behaviour of MPs needed to be above reproach with no whiff of scandal or personal impropriety. With only one case of a ministerial resignation in 1940, the Menzies years were noteworthy for their relative absence of ministerial misconduct. While accepting that parliament could be a forum for heated sparring between political foes, he understood that a culture of personal respect between opponents was also essential for dispelling recurrent public cynicism of parliamentary politics. Menzies believed that friendly and courteous relations between members of opposing sides ultimately made for stronger debate and good order. As in matters of personal propriety, Menzies led by example, enjoying cordial relations with Labor leaders John Curtin and Ben Chifley as well as cultivating warm friendships with Labor's Fred Daly and Joe Gander. Menzies' adherence to parliamentary decorum and his esteem for the institution was noted by his biographer, A W Martin:

> He had a profound respect for the gravitas and etiquette of Parliament. He considered good speaking essential to the health of parliamentary proceedings, which he thought could too easily be reduced to a predictable charade by the exigencies of party discipline. In his view what happened in parliament was more than a mere pantomime.

As both the corpus of political life and the expression of democracy, the parliament for Menzies was the institutional fulcrum for a civilised and free society.

In addition to maintaining the integrity of parliament, Menzies had much to say about the art of politics more broadly. While he always regarded the law as his 'first love', it was in the realm of politics where Menzies made his mark as a consummate parliamentarian and world statesman. For Menzies, politics was no mere occupation but an art and science developed over centuries that concerned itself with the great questions of parliamentarianism, statecraft, democracy, the contest of philosophical principles, the character of society and the welfare of the individual citizen. Rising above the cult of personality and the fortnightly-round of opinion polls, politics was about big-minded, public-spirited men and women devoting their character, talents and energies to the betterment of their nation. The essence of statesmanship for Menzies was not simply the ability to win elections and manage the media cycle but about having the vision to communicate ideas, formulate policy and inspire citizens to build a better future for their country.

For politics to be effective, Menzies believed that it needed to be an eminently practical enterprise. Rather than being preoccupied merely with doctrinaire theories of philosophy and economics, it had to be concerned with the day-to-day lives of ordinary men and women. To be sure, it was necessary for politicians to be grounded in philosophical principles with a clear understanding of parliament, a close knowledge of history and some knowledge of the broad principles of economics, but they also needed to understand the practical implications of their ideas and how to execute these as effective policy measures for the nation. Citing the example of former US President Woodrow Wilson, Menzies lauded the Great War leader for his faculties as 'an intellectual, a scholar and a thinker', but observed that his approach was 'too academic' in failing 'to take the ordinary people of the United States with him'. For politicians to be able to carry the electorate with them, it was essential for them to clearly communicate their ideas to the people, and if possible, to persuade a majority to agree. Menzies singled out another US President, Franklin D Roosevelt, as an exemplar for his mastery of communication and ability to convince the American people to eventually support the Allied war effort. In short, effective politics for Menzies was about mastering both the science of knowledge and the art of public persuasion.

The vocation of politics for Menzies was not primarily one of personal development, professional advance or pecuniary gain but one of unselfish service to the community and nation. Menzies emphasised that the political office of 'minister' was one of a 'servant' bound to do what was best for the country as a whole. Eschewing populism, Menzies argued that public service was not about doing what was most popular but doing what was right for the country. The question to be asked behind every decision made in politics was whether a given policy or programme would serve to improve the living standards of citizens and contribute to their happiness and wellbeing. For Menzies the rationale for serving in politics was to make Australia a more prosperous, secure, free, educated, humane, just and fair society. Famously declaring that he would govern not only for those who voted for him but also those who voted against him, Menzies repudiated the politics of sectionalism to emphasise that his government for all Australians would transcend the barriers of sectarianism, racialism, national and class hostility. Menzies saw his involvement in politics as a public service, and politics as an activity whose purpose was to advance the interests of the community as a whole. Politics should never be seen as a selfish activity to better oneself, or to promote some special interest at the community's expense, but to improve the lives of all.

"I protest, and will continue to protest, against this constant desire which exists in some quarters to sectionalise the community, to divide it up into this group and that group, and then to say, 'What group are you barracking for?'"

Robert Menzies, Address as President of the United Australia Organisation at the First Annual Conference, 21 September, 1932

"In every parliament represented today we are conscious of our responsibility; we are proud of the instrument that has been fashioned and passed on to us; and we are thoroughly determined that by no fault of our own shall the English System of Parliamentary Government perish from the earth"

Robert Menzies, Address in Great Hall, Houses of Parliament, London, 4 July 1935

"In our own case, we adhere to parliamentary rule because in a more or less ill-defined fashion we feel that the chief end of totalitarianism is to glorify power and enjoy it forever while the chief end of democracy is the achievement and development of individual freedom"

Robert Menzies, Freedom in Modern Society, 1935

"The democratic system is really built up upon debate, and the proper debating of a question takes us right back to what has been called the Socratic method of question and answer. Parliament itself is the chief debating society of the realm, and those who see in its methods only vain repetition and a waste of time have failed to appreciate that it is in the course of full and open debate that the solid truth is disposed to emerge"

Robert Menzies, Political Campaigning Broadcast, 3 September 1943

"If we are to win anything from a football match to a war, we must organise our forces. We must have team work. We must have leadership and loyalty. We cannot expect each of us just to play our own game"

Robert Menzies, Five Minutes Broadcast, 1945

"It is a good thing for Parliament that its members should be organised into large, powerful and responsible parties"

Robert Menzies, Five Minutes Broadcast, 1945

"John Curtin was my friend…He was a strenuous fighter for what he believed to be right, but he was a fair fighter. He possessed a rare political judgment, a noble sense of devotion to the national cause, a willingness to work to the point of exhaustion in the duties of his office, and a kindliness of nature which made their impact upon the public mind and conscience and at the end have left Australia his lasting debtor"

Robert Menzies, Broadcast in honour of the late Prime Minister, Mr Curtin, 5 July 1945

"We need to return to politics as a clash of principles, and to get away from the notion that it is a clash only of warring personalities"
Robert Menzies, Election Speech, 20 August 1946

"The powers and responsibilities of Parliament require constant watchfulness on the part of the Australian people"
Robert Menzies, Election Speech, 20 August 1946

"The truly representative character of Parliament as the great forum of the nation and the effective maker and controller of the nation's laws and administration is vital to British democracy. Men have died for it before now. We shall lose our living faith in it at our peril. It is the one precious element which dignifies the office of the private citizen, which ensures his ordered freedom, and which guarantees him protection against unscrupulous careerists and ambitious tyrants"
Robert Menzies, The Banking Bill (1947), Second Reading Speech, House of Representatives, 23 October 1947

"I believe that politics is the most important and responsible civil activity to which a man may devote his character, his talents, and his energy. We must, in our own interests, elevate politics into statesmanship and statecraft"
Robert Menzies, Politics as an Art, New York Times Magazine, 28 November 1948

"The business of political warfare is not to destroy your opponent, but to defeat him"
Robert Menzies, Politics as an Art, New York Time Magazine, 28 November 1948

"Do not imagine for one moment that Parliaments exist only for making Acts of Parliament. Parliaments exist for leadership, for the expression of opinion at the highest level, for the concentration of ideas, for the exchange of thought, for the total raising of the level of public knowledge and public judgment"
Robert Menzies, Speech at Wesley Church, Melbourne, 4 September 1949

"Politics can be a hard business. The more strongly you hold your own views, the more strenuously must you fight your political opponent. In a sense, you must strike, and spare not. Yet underneath this conflict there are in public life warm personal friendships between political foes; friendships which serve to sweeten life; friendships which endure beyond death"

Robert Menzies, Broadcast following the death of the Leader of the Opposition, the Rt Hon J B Chifley, 14 June 1951

"He [Ben Chifley] had in abundance those human qualities of easy informality, of deep conviction, of quiet humour, and of engaging frankness which made him, in the old phrase, 'a man's man'...He set a high example of great ability, and devotion, and industry. He was a good Australian. He was a good man"

Robert Menzies, Broadcast following the death of the Leader of the Opposition, the Rt Hon J B Chifley, 14 June 1951

"Parliament is our great expression of democracy. Parliament is both an instrument of reasoned progress, largely because there are both Government and Opposition; the hammer and the anvil, forging ideas and making laws. And parliament cannot work as it should unless between Prime Minister and Opposition Leader there is to be found courtesy, mutual consideration and respect, a common belief in the importance of the functions of each"

Robert Menzies, Broadcast following the death of the Leader of the Opposition, the Rt Hon J B Chifley, 14 June 1951

"No government can please everybody, because many pressure groups are in conflict with one another. And a government should not try to please everybody, for it ought to have principles and a mind of its own. The ultimate responsibility of a government is to do what it thinks is best for the nation as a whole"

Robert Menzies, 'Australia Today – Man to Man', Broadcast, 16 September 1953

"The existence of Local Government as we know it is vital to the good government of the nation...I think it would be bad if we centralised power; and that the nearer a particular problem is to the ordinary daily life of the citizens, the nearer to him should be the authority which deals with it."

Robert Menzies, 'Australia Today – Man to Man', Broadcast, 11 November 1953

"If public life is merely a job, Parliament will become full of job-holders and job seekers. If we all have to be paid for every piece of social duty that we perform, than the true spirit of social service will disappear. These are the real reasons why local government in Australia, evoking as it does, the decent and unselfish service of local men and women, is essentially not only mechanically but spiritually to Australian democracy"

Robert Menzies, 'Australia Today – Man to Man', Broadcast, 11 November 1953

"Whatever party we belong to we should genuinely aim at doing what is in the long run best for the country. And that requires not ill-tempered and abusive election campaigns but conflicts of honest opinion"

Robert Menzies, 'Australia Today – Man to Man', Broadcast, 17 March 1954

"The conception of politics which divides it into a series of pressure groups pushing their own interests is disastrous. That a man should be concerned about his own personal affairs is natural, and I have no complaint to make about it. But surely every one of us should prefer the interests of the nation to his own"

Robert Menzies, 'Australia Today – Man to Man', Broadcast, 17 March 1954

"A political leader must not lose sight of either the past or the present. But he must also have in mind a lively picture of the future. So it is not only a matter of considering the past and the immediate present; it is a matter of considering the future. And this means that a man has not merely to think of his children or his grand-children as the objects of his affection but as the

objects of his responsibility"

Robert Menzies, 'Australia Today – Man to Man', Broadcast, 14 April 1954

"I don't enjoy this talk about 'bread and butter' policies. Bread becomes stale and butter becomes rancid. Each has to be eaten fairly quickly. A nation which voted only on 'bread and butter' issues would find itself with a different administration and policy and set of principles every three years"

Robert Menzies, 'Australia Today – Man to Man', Broadcast, 14 April 1954

"The truth remains that, if we concentrate on our differences and forget our unities, politics will sound and be like a civil war. The one thing that the bitter and narrow partisans forget is the continuity of national security and growth requires, on great matters, a certain continuity of policy. We secure that by remembering our unities; we destroy it by thinking only of our differences"

Robert Menzies, The First William Queale Memorial Lecture, Adelaide, 22 October 1954

"Amongst decent people around the world the elements of unity are immeasurably greater than the elements of disunity"

Robert Menzies, Speeches in Honour of R G Menzies, 5 March 1955

"It was a common experience for me to be told by bankers or by doctors or by many other people of various groups and occupations that they took no interest in politics. More than once I remember replying that the day would come when politics would take an interest in them"

Robert Menzies, Arthur E Mills Memorial Oration, Sydney, 11 May 1955

"A member of parliament has a very great duty to his people, and one of those duties…is to bring to the service of the country their own judgment and industry and character, not distorted by anybody else's opinion at all, with the sure knowledge, of course, that if what they do, if what they say they stand for, if what their judgment

requires them to decide at some particular point does not commend themselves to the electors they will be out"

Robert Menzies, Speech at St Mark's Library Canberra, 27 August 1959

"I am a Prime Minister of Australia and there is a national parliament in Australia, and there is a parliament in each state capital, and a Premier and Ministers, because hundreds of years ago our forefathers in Great Britain sat under the village oak tree and learned how to manage their own affairs, their own public affairs, their own local government. Step by step, over centuries the position was achieved in which there was a Parliament elected freely by all the adult people in the country without regard to wealth or privilege. That didn't happen overnight"

Robert Menzies, Speech to Central Methodist Mission, 6 September 1959

"He [the statesman] must communicate his ideas, to a Cabinet, to Parliament, to the people. He must do this as well as he possibly can. His language must be such as to arrest and sustain interest, He must not condescend. He must seek to instruct, to explain, and to inspire. The vocabulary he employs must be rich and flexible. He must not under-estimate the public by thinking that the common-place is good enough"

Robert Menzies, The Challenge of Education, 19 May 1961

"The essential quality of good government is that it should have sound and intelligible principles, that it should pursue great national and social objectives with resoluteness, that it should be able to meet the storms that arise from time to time with a proper sense of navigation, that it should have cohesion in its own ranks and a strong sense of mutual loyalty"

Robert Menzies, Policy Speech, Kew, 15 November 1961

"The art of politics is that of achieving the attainable, not of seeking vainly to achieve perfection in one stroke. To take a few steps forward in what they believe to be the right direction is all that most political leaders may hope for"

Robert Menzies, The John Storey Memorial Lecture, Melbourne, 8 December 1962

"President Kennedy had great courage, ability and personal attraction. He had already made a notable mark on world events and on the relations between the Soviet Union and the Western World"

Robert Menzies, Death of President Kennedy, Sydney, 23 November 1963

"You must have a proper respect for politicians, but you must also have a certain healthy distrust for us. We're not always to be entrusted with great power. It's a very good thing to have a division of power, if you're going to preserve liberty. Give any political organisation full power, and you are taking the first step in the direction of a tyranny"

Robert Menzies, Speech to Federation of Parents and Citizens Associations of NSW, 14 August 1964

"When they say a man is a great parliamentarian, you must never think that means he has been in parliament a long time. It means that he knows every noise and every creak in the machinery and he understands the human beings who are in Parliament and is able to proceed without becoming involved in avoidable arguments or talking himself out of his own Bill"

Robert Menzies, National Press Club Luncheon, 14 September 1964

"A good parliament cannot exist without good members. A good parliament cannot exist without good debate - strong debate, strenuous debate and, every now and then, if you like, heated debate. But we all know from our experience that when the debates are over we look round the House and we on each side of the House know that we have a lot of close personal friends among our political opponents. This is as it should be"

R. G. Menzies, House of Representatives, 10 December 1965

"The duty of an Opposition, if it has no ambition to be permanently on the left-hand side of the Speaker, is not to just oppose for opposition's sake, but to oppose selectively. No Government is always wrong on everything, whatever the critics may say. The Opposition must choose the ground on which it is to attack. To attack indiscriminately is to risk public opinion, which has a reserve of fairness not always understood"

Robert Menzies, Afternoon Light, 1967, p 15

"Opposition, with few administrative duties, gives more time for study and thought. It must be regarded as a great constructive period in the life of a party; properly considered, not a period in the wilderness, but a period of preparation for the high responsibilities which you hope will come"

Robert Menzies, Afternoon Light, 1967, p 17

"The greatest academic political scientist in the country, could, in practical politics, involve both himself and his electors in complete disaster, unless he had learned and understood the art of politics, which involves the persuasion and management of men"

Robert Menzies, 'The Science and Art of Politics', University of Texas Lectures (No 1), 20 November 1969

"The art of politics is to convey ideas to others, if possible, to persuade a majority to agree; to create or encourage a public opinion so soundly based that it endures, and is not blown aside by chance winds; to persuade people to take long-range views"

Robert Menzies, 'The Science and Art of Politics', University of Texas Lectures (No 1), 20 November 1969

"If an honest, talented man of great affairs can approach the end of his days and feel able to say to himself, in the still watches of the night, that he has done his best to master the scientific aspects of his politics and to practise the great art of politics for the benefit of his people, he can rest content. In the long run, he will not be judged exclusively by his enemies, but by the decent common sense of a free people"

Robert Menzies, 'The Science and Art of Politics', University of Texas Lectures (No 1), 20 November 1969

"A political party must never be a party which chronically says 'No'. If it never loses sight of its own ideas, it will be positive and creative. It must consistently formulate and fight for its own ideas, and never let either the people or its opponents remain ignorant of what those ideas are"

Robert Menzies, Inaugural Sir Robert Menzies Lecture,

Perth, 12 May 1970

"The great hope of the world in this century has always come back to the people who had a Parliamentary democracy which meant that their Parliaments spoke of their people and had a strength derived from their people"

Robert Menzies, Australia-Britain Society Inaugural Dinner, Sydney, 26 August 1971

"The further truth is, of course, that the best guarantee of human rights in the future, is to be found in our system of responsible government, where Ministers sit in Parliament, can be questioned, and give answers, and the Government itself may be turned out if Parliament feels that it is doing things which violate the proper rights of individuals"

Robert Menzies, 'Civil and Political Rights', Article for Melbourne Herald, 13-15 March 1974

"Statesmanship in modern political practice requires that the long view should be taken. It is not a matter of what tomorrow's newspaper may say, but a matter of how the country will feel in a year's time if some particular policy is adopted"

Robert Menzies, Statement on the media in public affairs, 26 March 1975

16

Religion and Faith

Fond of describing himself as a 'simple Presbyterian', Menzies had inherited a strong tradition of Scots Presbyterianism from his father's side of the family. However, when James Menzies had settled in Jeparit with wife Kate in 1893, there was no Presbyterian Church so the elder Menzies joined the Methodist fold and became a trustee and lay preacher of the Jeparit Methodist Church. It was into this religious environment that Robert Menzies was born with regular church-going and Bible reading forming a part of his early upbringing. At University, he maintained his religiosity and served as President of the Melbourne University Students' Christian Union in 1916. Under the influence of C H Nash, who later became Principal of the Melbourne Bible Institute, Menzies adopted the habit of daily Bible reading. As Menzies embarked on his legal career at the Bar in the 1920s, he occasionally worshipped at Melbourne's Kew Presbyterian Church with his wife Pattie who shared his Scottish Presbyterian roots.

Throughout his lengthy career in politics, Menzies exhibited signs of the religious faith he had imbibed from childhood and early adulthood. Peppered with phrases and aphorisms from Christian scripture such as 'my brother's keeper' and 'a house of many mansions', his speeches espoused what he esteemed as the middle-class Protestant values of personal integrity, thrift, industry, domestic propriety and community service. The most frequent platform on which Menzies discussed moral and religious themes was the routine 'Pleasant Sunday Afternoon' address at Melbourne's Wesley (Methodist) Church. The Superintendent of

Wesley Church from 1935-1967, Sir Clarence Irving Benson, became a personal friend of Menzies and shared his political outlook. Along with R G (Lord) Casey, Menzies was regularly invited to appear at Benson's Pleasant Sunday Afternoons where he would often speak on the moral and spiritual challenges to Western civilisation posed by Cold War communism and materialism. The religious views of Menzies had also surfaced in his keynote *Forgotten People* broadcast of 1942. His stated philosophy that 'Human nature is greatest when it combines dependence upon God with independence of man' revealed much about his understanding of God *vis-à-vis* humanity. From his Protestant upbringing, he had imbibed the view that human beings were imperfect and needed to rely upon God for moral guidance and redemption. As a liberal, however, he also embraced the Scottish Enlightenment's belief in human progress which held that men and women possessed the innate potential to independently seek self-improvement through education and the cultivation of civilised habits.

True to his own epithet as a 'simple Presbyterian', Menzies' personal brand of Protestantism was theologically uncomplicated and essentially practical with an emphasis on self-giving service. Like the twentieth-century Anglican writer and apologist, C S Lewis, Menzies would have viewed himself as an exponent of 'mere Christianity' which rejected atheism to affirm the Christian basics of a Trinitarian God, a divinely inspired Bible and personal redemption through Christ while downplaying the significance of theological differences between the denominations and branches of Christianity. Viewing the Bible as the common wellspring of faith for Christians of all churches, Menzies observed that it was 'better to seek the fountainhead than to divide up amongst the little streams'. Menzies believed that it was infinitely more constructive for the Church, as a whole, to focus on preaching a common gospel and seeking to enrich the community through good works than to be inwardly preoccupied with settling finer points of doctrine. He had a particularly high esteem for the practical Christianity of churches such as the Salvation Army and the Central Methodist Missions of Melbourne and Sydney. In his own

Presbyterian Church, he identified closely with the Rev Dr J Fred McKay, the successor to Rev John Flynn of the Royal Flying Doctor Service. Regarding McKay as a personal friend and spiritual confidante, he admired the clergyman as a 'good, practical Christian'.

While proud of his Scottish Presbyterian roots and committed to preserving Australia's Christian heritage, not least of all its church schools, Menzies recognised the diversity of the nation's faith communities and therefore preached religious freedom and non-sectarianism as the norm for Australia in the 1950s and 60s. Abhorring sectarian animosity as repugnant to both liberal and Christian principles, Menzies had a long track-record of seeking to heal the Catholic-Protestant rift that had long blighted Australian society. In 1928, he defended his decision to attend the opening of a Catholic school in his electorate of East Yarra amid opposition from some of his constituents. As the Victorian Attorney-General in the early 1930s, he attracted criticism for standing up to Protestant efforts to ban a large Catholic Eucharistic procession through the streets of central Melbourne. As Prime Minister in 1939, he addressed a Melbourne peace rally organised by the Australian National Secretariat for Catholic Action and stressed the shared faith of all present by drawing attention to his presence, as a Presbyterian, on a Catholic platform.

In Menzies' second period as Prime Minister, his cooperation with Australian Catholics on the contentious state aid issue was recognised when he was invited as guest of honour to the annual Cardinal's Dinner in Sydney 1964, presided over by Cardinal Norman Gilroy. As well as building bridges with Catholics, Menzies enjoyed an excellent rapport with Australia's Jewish community. He deeply respected the Jewish legacy for its profound contribution to Western civilisation and admired the Jewish people for their cultural traditions of scholarship, civic-mindedness and enduring sense of kinship. Frequently invited to speak at ceremonies organised by the Jewish community, Menzies praised the Jewish people for their contribution to Australia. At the Cardinal's dinner, he told his audience that citizens of all faiths were part of Australia and had a duty to serve the country to the best of their talents.

With his pronouncements as Prime Minister seldom touching upon the specifics of religious doctrine, Menzies nonetheless affirmed that the Judeo-Christian ethic was fundamental to both the character of civilisation and the survival of human freedom. Like liberal statesmen such as Edmund Burke and Abraham Lincoln, he appreciated the indebtedness of modern democracy to the Judeo-Christian inheritance and the Enlightenment. From his own keen sense of history, he understood that the disastrous attempts of both the French and Bolshevik Revolutions to crush the religious freedom of the people had led to tyranny and oppression. For Menzies, the twentieth-century represented a depressing catalogue of strife and war in which the triumph of pagan ideologies had served to grievously disfigure human civilisation. As the antidote to the 'soulless materialism' propagated by either Marxism or Fascism, Menzies espoused a Christian-inspired liberalism, not dissimilar to that of European-style Christian democracy, which stressed first, the relationship of human beings to 'their maker' and the 'divine and spiritual law', and second, the relationship of human beings to one another as 'members of one body'. Given that this political creed was not doctrinally-specific in its enunciation, it could be accepted by citizens of all faiths in a society such as Australia.

"We must re-assert the truth, that materialism is not enough. Man does not live by bread alone. A slavery to the gods of material well-being is a degrading slavery. We have inherited great spiritual traditions of unselfish service"
Robert Menzies, Freedom in Modern Society, 1935

"Human nature is at its greatest when it combines dependence upon God with independence of man"
Robert Menzies, The Forgotten People Speech, 22 May 1942

"Just as the Bible taught the English their own English so it wove into the fabric of the English character that profound realisation of the existence of God, that profound belief in the value of the

moral judgment that has made our race the greatest race in the world, and that alone can keep our race a great race"

Robert Menzies, The Oldest Book with the Newest Message, 15 July 1940

"Our judgment has been a judgment founded upon an appreciation of the moral nature of man, and not merely a judgment of expediency founded upon the strength or the weakness of our opponents"

Robert Menzies, The Oldest Book with the Newest Message, 15 July 1940

"All things that our Faith stands for — quiet living and human kindness, the freedom of the soul, justice to our neighbours, the essential brotherhood of man, are today challenged and nothing less than our best can save them from eclipse"

Robert Menzies, Election Speech, 2 September 1940

"The religious freedom for which the Scottish Covenanters fought was freedom for all, Catholic or Protestant, Jew or Gentile, and that to deny it was to go back to the dark ages of man. Religious persecution was the denial of freedom. Freedom of worship is the victorious enemy of persecution"

Robert Menzies, Freedom of Worship, Broadcast, 3 July 1942

"We are a diversity of creatures, with a diversity of minds and emotions and imaginations and faiths. When we claim freedom of worship we claim room and respect for all"

Robert Menzies, Freedom of Worship, Broadcast, 3 July 1942

"Sectarian strife is the enemy of freedom or worship, not its friend. It is the denial of Christianity not its proof"

Robert Menzies, Freedom of Worship, Broadcast, 3 July 1942

"The Cross which is the symbol of the Christian faith is itself the figure of sacrifice"

Robert Menzies, Christmas Night Broadcast, 25 December 1942

"Christianity…begins its teaching by imposing on every citizen the obligation of unselfishness, of thinking of the interests of his neighbour before his own, and regarding himself as his brother's keeper"

Robert Menzies, The Christian Citizen in a New Era, St Columba Presbyterian Church, Woollahra, NSW, 27 February 1944

"If ever man has set up a golden calf to worship, it is in the last forty-years or so, when he has been worshipping at the shrine of his own diabolical cleverness, and because he has become so great a worshipper of the material, the world has been rocked into such ruinous disaster."

Robert Menzies, The Christian Citizen in a New Era, St Columba Presbyterian Church, Woollahra, NSW, 27 February 1944

"You see, the greatest problem of the world is not to discover how fast you may travel from one part of the globe to another, but to expand the heart and nature of man, and how you may extend your duties to another man, and how above all, we may understand our duty to our Maker."

Robert Menzies, The Christian Citizen in a New Era, St Columba Presbyterian Church, Woollahra, NSW, 27 February 1944

"I believe that religion gives to people a sensitive understanding of their obligations and that is something which the world sadly needs at the present time."

Robert Menzies, Education, Parliamentary Debates, House of Representatives, 26 July 1945

"The Christian faith is one of love, and rejects hatred of human beings as an instrument of true human progress"

R. G. Menzies, Christianity and Communism, Broadcast, 1946

"The whole essence of the Sermon on the Mount is that you must be prepared to do more than the Law commands, and that means that you are not to concern yourself only with the letter but concern yourself with the spirit"

Robert Menzies, 'Address on Christianity and Law', St Stephen's Forum, 15 December 1946

"It would be a barren theologian who thought that the religion of Christ was concerned with the letter. It is concerned exclusively with the spirit. It issues its orders not to the mind of man but to the conscience of man, to that immortal part of man which does not depend upon final interpretation but which depends upon its adjustment to the laws of God and its adjustment to the rights, the interests, properly understood, of all other human beings"

Robert Menzies, 'Address on Christianity and Law', St Stephen's Forum, 15 December 1946

"If in the course of self-government we are to make our temporal law more and more Christian in its form and application then we will have to get over the idea that the commands that men lay upon men, if performed, are sufficient; we will have to go into this strange, difficult doctrine, this marvellous teaching so almost impossible of human performance that we find in the Sermon on the Mount"

Robert Menzies, 'Address on Christianity and Law', St Stephen's Forum, 15 December 1946

"Every man is above all a spirit; man is a spiritual animal"

Robert Menzies, Freedom and the Call to Action, Lecture to Junior Chamber of Commerce, 4 August 1947

"The civilised world saw in the establishment of Israel not only the providing of an independent home for many Jewish people but also a shining symbol of delivery from bondage, and (I believe) of world repentance"

Robert Menzies on the recognition of the State of Israel, 1949

"I speak of the 70 000 Jews in Australia not only in Australia, but of Australia. For here, you are not, and should not be, a race apart. In this free country, all are free; all are equal before the

law; religious or sectional prejudices tend 'to fade into the light of common day'"

R. G. Menzies on the recognition of the State of Israel, 1949

"The great Jewish contribution to Australia is not sectional or sectarian but a community contribution, neither discriminating nor being discriminated against. It is your historic function and destiny to enrich the Australian character by making your special contribution to the whole composite body. Isaacs and Monash - enduring and honoured names. Jews they were; but they are honoured as great Australians"

R. G. Menzies on the recognition of the State of Israel, 1949

"The one man, for he was human as well as divine, whose memory holds no blemish, whose influence has grown for nearly two thousand years, whose birthday is the occasion for rejoicing for hundreds of millions of men and women, was and is Jesus Christ"

Robert Menzies, 'Australia Today – Man to Man', Broadcast, 23 December 1953

"The most important thing in the world, may I say for myself, is man's relation to his maker: his relation to the divine and spiritual law. The second most important thing is man's relation to man, with all that it implies of brotherhood and understanding and fair play and responsibility. The third is man's scientific and mechanical skill, and the extension of the boundaries of knowledge."

Robert Menzies, 'Australia Today – Man to Man', Broadcast, 17 March 1954

"We must reassert the truth, that materialism is not enough. Man does not live by bread alone. A slavery to the gods of material well-being is a degrading slavery. We have inherited great spiritual traditions of unselfish service."

Robert Menzies, The First William Queale Memorial Lecture, Adelaide, 22 October 1954

"It is grimly significant that the century which has seen the greatest scientific advancements of recorded history has been, more than perhaps any other, disfigured, not only by wars of a stupendous

range and intensity and destruction, but by widespread attacks upon the religion of love by organised hatreds and cruelties of the most barbarous kind"

Robert Menzies, Address to the Tenth Session of the Australasian Medical Congress, Hobart, 5 March 1958

"In my father's house there are many mansions. Don't forget it. There is room in every political party for Christian men and women of all schools of Christian thought"

Robert Menzies, Farewell to Dr Rayward, Sydney, 30 March, 1958

"I don't think we ought to be seeking to express Christianity in party political terms but I am perfectly certain that it's the duty of all of us to examine our own politics in Christian terms. These are two entirely different ideas"

Robert Menzies, Farewell to Dr Rayward, Sydney, 30 March, 1958

"Politics must still regard itself as pursuing policies, which while they may be economically quite different, while they may give rise to financial controversies, international arguments,   must not in themselves be anti-Christian policies or non-Christian policies. Therefore, it's right, that we should all in a country like this, constantly test our politics, constantly try our political faith by seeing that we express it in Christian terms but that doesn't mean that we can't disagree about politics. That doesn't mean that to be a good Christian you have to be a good Liberal or a good Country Party man, or a good Labor man. I'm saying exactly the opposite. To be a good Liberal, to be a good Labor man, to be a good Country Party man, you will be all the better if you are a Christian"

Robert Menzies, Farewell to Dr Rayward, Sydney, 30 March, 1958

"I know that in the course of history there have been divisions in the Christian Church, and for some reasons that seemed good to somebody or other, we among Protestants, Anglicans or Presbyterians or Methodists or Congregationalists or Baptists.

And no doubt we all have some differences among ourselves in terms of government; sometimes in some point of doctrine. But I always like to feel that underneath all this there is one Bible, there is one message; and that the nearer we get to that, the less we will be concerned with dogma of any kind"

Robert Menzies, Speech at Salvation Army Citizens' Rally, Melbourne, March 22, 1959

"There is a long history in Australia of distinguished service to our country by Jewish citizens. The Jews in Australia are good Australians. Any attempt to create an anti-Jewish feeling in Australia is doomed to failure"

Robert Menzies, 'Anti-Semitism in Australia', Canberra, 26 January 1960

"The Bible is the most remarkable repository of religious history. Frankly, I don't think that any man could regard himself as educated unless he had become familiar with the great historic stories of the Bible"

Robert Menzies, Official Opening National Memorial Bible House, Canberra, 13 February 1960

"The Bible is the repository of our faith and of our inspiration. Never out of date, always up to date, always difficult of application and therefore stimulating to thoughtful people. It is the great source of faith, and of course that is why we ought to read it...The story is there, the great history is there, the great gospel is there, the whole spirit of Christianity is there"

Robert Menzies, Official Opening National Memorial Bible House, Canberra, 13 February 1960

"If I were, as I am not, an atheist or an agnostic or some other such unhappy person I would still take the Bible with me to a desert island for two reasons. One, that I would have a noble piece of literature to accompany me and two, because given ample opportunity to study it I might cease to be an atheist or an agnostic"

Robert Menzies, Official Opening National Memorial Bible House, Canberra, 13 February 1960

"Disfigured as the history of Europe is by the treatment of the Jews over centuries, it may I think be safely said that no disfigurement of that kind occurs or will occur in Australia"

Robert Menzies, Opening Speech at Mount Scopus College, Burwood Victoria, 13 September 1960

"I don't know of any group in the community which preserves its character, its family character, its intimate association, its own prides and its own faith, while at the same time, being so integrally bound up with the community as a whole. Nobody can ever say, and I hope nobody ever will; that the Jewish community is a separatist body, that it lives to itself, that it lets the world go by. That's not at all true; the fact is that you have made a great contribution to the current life of Australia. And that is a magnificent reconciliation, to reconcile your group pride, faith, fashions, emotions; with the general service of the country"

Robert Menzies, Opening Speech at Mount Scopus College, Burwood Victoria, 13 September 1960

"In the long run we may have clever citizens, ingenious citizens, even brave citizens, but unless they are citizens whose character has been enriched by the background of religious training they will not be the best citizens for Australia"

Robert Menzies, Opening Speech at Mount Corpus College, Burwood Victoria, 13 September 1960

"That just as freedom is not easily beaten out of the heart of man, so is faith not easily beaten out of him. You cannot take thousands, millions, hundreds of millions of people who have a faith of their own, and destroy it, merely by order or command"

Robert Menzies, Second Freedom Rally, Melbourne, 5 November 1960

"When God made man in His own image, He wasn't creating something necessarily that had a physical resemblance to Him. He was creating something that had the God-like elements in the spirit and in the character"

Robert Menzies, Civic Service, Presbyterian Church, Cheltenham, Victoria, 4 April 1965

"If we are in His image, it is because we have within us a capacity for rising to great heights of pure virtue, side by side with a capacity for sinking to the lowest level of selfishness and bitterness; but these God-like elements in the human character, sometimes twisted sometimes ignored, I believe survive and blossom and develop as life goes on"

Robert Menzies, Civic Service, Presbyterian Church, Cheltenham, Victoria, 4 April 1965

"This capacity for sacrifice, this capacity for preferring other people to oneself, this capacity for saying, I will contribute all if it is for the good of the country, exhibited so frequently in war is a God-like quality. The capacity for sacrifice, the whole idea of sacrifice is at the very root of the Christian faith"

Robert Menzies, Civic Service, Presbyterian Church, Cheltenham, Victoria, 4 April 1965

17

Family

For Menzies, the family played a pre-eminent role in guaranteeing the welfare of the individual. According to Margaret Fitzherbert, the home and family were central to the Menzies Government's broader agenda. This was scarcely surprising given the emphasis Menzies placed on the family in his *Forgotten People* Address, where he described the home 'as the foundation of sanity and sobriety' and extolled the virtues of 'homes material, homes human and homes spiritual'. For Menzies, the impersonal welfare rendered by detached state bureaucracies was simply no substitute for the personalised care and kinship of family. Menzies understood that it was the family, rather than the state, to which children instinctively turned to for the provision of their basic needs. The family, however, fulfilled a dual purpose in not only nurturing the dependent child but fostering the emergence of the independent adult. For Menzies, the family home was the sphere in which growing children would be encouraged to become 'lifters rather than leaners'. It was within this primary matrix of intimate human relationships that children would first learn the lesson of being 'their brother's keeper', a phrase frequently invoked by Menzies in his speeches. The family, in short, was where persons acquired the habits of self-discipline, personal responsibility towards others and independence. Personal attributes that Menzies regarded as essential to the health and survival of human civilisation. The strengthening and protection of the family unit was thus the key to realising his vision of a sturdily self-reliant yet interdependent citizenry. To strengthen and support the family, Menzies and his government introduced some practical policy initiatives including child endowment, home-ownership incentives and family tax benefits.

In his first significant measure to assist Australian families, Menzies and his government initiated the scheme of child endowment in 1941.[10] Under the *Child Endowment Act* 1941 (Cth), the government paid child endowment directly to the mother, at a flat rate of five shillings per week for each child *after* the first under the age of 16 years. The provision was not subject to any means test and nor was it taxable. Esteeming the family as a supreme social good which was indispensable to human happiness and wellbeing, the government maintained that it was essential for a free enterprise economy such as Australia's to invest in 'persons' as well as 'things'. Thus if governments could justify investing in social goods such as education, there was every reason for them to support the family unit through a scheme of child endowment. Following his return to the Prime Ministership in 1949, Menzies expanded his government's original 1941 child endowment scheme. In a progressive move, child endowment payments – paid to mothers of all children other than the first, and up to the age of sixteen – were extended to include the first child. Accordingly, payments of five shillings per week for a first child aged less than 16 years were introduced while child endowment for the second and each additional child continued at 10 shillings per week.

Appreciating that his 'homes human' and 'homes spiritual' needed to of course dwell in 'homes physical', Menzies and his Government regarded the provision of accessible housing as integral to buttressing the family. Responding to the housing shortages evident during the Depression and Second World War, the Menzies Government devised several ways to stimulate the outright ownership of homes using the leverage of public funding and regulatory policies.[11] In a nod to both free enterprise and the family, the Menzies Government encouraged the States to sell their public housing stock to prospective private purchasers on credit terms, rather than keeping this in government hands. Within four years, more than 75% of the houses being built each year under the Commonwealth-State

Housing Agreement were sold to family purchasers. In a further initiative to facilitate home ownership, the Government provided cash payments in 1964 under a Home Savings Grants Scheme, easing the constraints experienced by young married couples under 36 seeking to purchase their first home. As well as facilitating marriage and family formation, the legislation was designed to encourage individual thrift with the incentive for young marrieds to save a portion of their personal income towards the acquisition of a property. Accordingly, the scheme required couples to have 'accumulated acceptable savings in Australia for at least three years' to be eligible for a Commonwealth grant of £1 for every £3 of savings for a home.[12]

In 1965, the Menzies government created the Housing Loans Insurance Corporation, encouraging institutional lenders to advance additional loans to homebuyers by insuring loans of up to 95% of the value of a house worth up to $15 000.[13] As well as providing a stable dwelling-place for family life to flourish, Menzies and his government saw home-ownership as the best security against future welfare dependency. Thus for Menzies, true and lasting social welfare was to be found not so much in government cash handouts but in accessible home-ownership where citizens could cultivate the habits of individual enterprise, thrift and personal responsibility for managing a house, garden and family. The impact of these policy initiatives by the post-war Menzies government was palpable with the rates of home-ownership amongst Australian families increasing from 53% in 1947 to 70% in 1961.[14]

As well as child endowment and housing, the other policy measure designed to assist the family was the system of tax deductions introduced in the 1950-51 budget. In opting for tax cuts rather than cash handouts, this initiative of the Menzies government to support families accorded with the Liberal instinct to provide due reward for enterprise and effort by giving wage-earners a tax break. The system of deductions allowed for an annual deduction from taxable income of £104 for a dependent spouse with a separate income of up to £52 per year, after which the deduction tapered off rapidly, reducing by £2 for every £1 earned. In addition, dependent children up to the age of 16 could be claimed as a tax deduction, as could dependent children between 16 and 19 years who were in full-time education. The financial values of the tax deductions were adjusted to retain most of their value against inflation.[15] While affirming the family as the primary mechanism for welfare support, Menzies recognised that in cases where lacunae existed in an individual's personal support network, the State had a legitimate role and indeed an obligation to intervene with appropriate welfare support. The chief end of such support, however, was always to protect the individual in a time of need and never to induce an attitude of indefinite dependence upon the State.

"The home is the foundation of sanity and sobriety; it is the indispensable condition of continuity; its health determines the health of society as a whole"

Robert Menzies, The Forgotten People Speech, 22 May 1942

"My home is where my wife and children are. The instinct to be with them is the great instinct of civilised man; the instinct to give them a chance in life – to make them not leaners but lifters – is a noble instinct"

Robert Menzies, The Forgotten People Speech, 22 May 1942

"The great question is, 'How can I qualify my son to help society?' Not, as we have so frequently thought, 'How can I qualify society to help my son?'"

Robert Menzies, The Forgotten People Speech, 22 May 1942

"We must get rid of this idea that the community has become so feeble-minded that it needs to have its homes built for it by huge Government Departments, the inflated cost of which will, of course, be built into the cost of every house erected by it"

Robert Menzies, Housing, Fremantle By-election, 15 August 1945

"In a free community, the family and the family spirit are not only the foundation of society but also the best guarantee of its quality and endurance"

Robert Menzies, General Elections 1955: Taxation on Company Profits, Broadcast, 17 November 1955

"It is our continuing policy to recognise the importance of the family; and we have done so at every possible opportunity, particularly by measures relating to taxation, health and education"

Robert Menzies, General Elections 1955: Taxation on Company Profits, Broadcast, 17 November 1955

"We need to build a home-owning nation if we are to preserve our traditions of sturdy independence"

Robert Menzies, 'Australia Today – Man to Man', Broadcast, 9 April 1958

"The family - a good family, a healthy family, a proud family, a family generous in itself - this is of the very essence of community life. There can be no great nations without great family feeling"

Robert Menzies, Opening of Jewish War Memorial Hall, Waverly [NSW], 7 February 1960

"That family feeling...which is at the very heart of a civilised community, that feeling of family responsibility, that willingness to do something for a brother or a sister, or a father or a mother, or an aunt or an uncle is a wonderful feeling, I wish we had more of it. One of the things that I occasionally worry myself about is the ease with which so many people are disposed to discard their family responsibilities in favour of the responsibilities of somebody else, putting it onto the State, putting it on to somebody else"

Robert Menzies, Opening Speech at Mount Corpus College, Burwood Victoria, 13 September 1960

"The family is the foundation of the nation, and those who have and bring up families are the nation's greatest contributing citizens"

Robert Menzies, Election Speech, 29 October 1958

18

Federalism

With his liberal beliefs in smaller government and the devolution of power, Menzies was an instinctive Federalist. Like the fathers of the American Constitution, Thomas Jefferson, James Madison and Alexander Hamilton, Menzies saw the division of government powers as serving to guarantee the individual a greater degree of liberty than that offered by a unitary system of government. With the machinery of Australian federalism already in place by Menzies' early boyhood, it was the system of government he familiarised himself with and operated in as a lawyer and politician. As a barrister specialising in Constitutional law, the legal cases he handled frequently dealt with questions of federalism, the most notable of these being the *Engineers Case* of 1920. Acting as counsel for the Amalgamated Society of Engineers, Menzies submitted that in this particular case there were constitutional grounds for extending the reach of Commonwealth power over the States. While not abandoning his instinct to protect State powers, he argued that the 'conciliation and arbitration' power under section 51 (xxxv) of the Constitution could authorise the Commonwealth Court of Arbitration and Conciliation to make a binding award for the engineers. Agreeing with Menzies' submission, the High Court held that the Commonwealth Court did have such power and so a new precedent was set for expanding the potential scope of Commonwealth power.

In spite of arguing for a greater reach of Commonwealth power in the

Engineers Case, Menzies respected Australia's federal system and was generally wary of excessive Commonwealth incursion on State juris-dictions. In his first foray into politics, Menzies campaigned against the Nationalist Bruce-Page Government's 1926 referendum to give the Commonwealth greater power over corporations, trade unions and in-dustrial disputes. Menzies joined a 'Federal Union' committee to support the 'No' case and appeared at meetings around Victoria to speak against the referendum. As Menzies dealt with successive Australian referenda that proposed extensions to Commonwealth power, his public posture varied. As Commonwealth Attorney-General in 1937, he supported, and indeed proposed, the referendum of the Lyons Government to give the Commonwealth legislative control over 'air navigation and aircraft'. In 1944, however, Menzies opposed Labor's 1944 referendum about giving the Commonwealth post-war legislative power. When the Chifley La-bor government in 1946 proposed three referendum questions to give the Commonwealth power over social services, marketing schemes and industrial relations, Menzies supported the social services amendment but opposed the other two.

Menzies' doctrine of Commonwealth and State powers could best be de-scribed as a pragmatic and balanced federalism. On the one hand, he de-fended the division of power and the important administrative functions of the individual States, but on the other hand, he stressed that the States were not sovereign powers unto themselves but rather constituent parts of a single nation with a common identity and a common destiny. To bal-ance these two principles, Menzies favoured a cooperative 'partnership' between the Commonwealth and the States in the administration of the country. Turning first to the merits of the States, Menzies saw these as necessary for functioning as checks on the concentration of power and its potential abuse. As desirable as it was to have a federal government which provided the country with the necessary leadership, direction and cohesion for it to flourish, the centralisation of too much power in Can-berra was to be avoided since this could make Australia more vulnera-ble to the rise of autocratic governments, whether communist or fascist.

Menzies' defence of the existing federalist arrangement was also based on the subsidiarity principle, the notion that the centres of power should be devolved to bring government closer to the people. In common with Catholic social doctrine, Menzies and the Liberal Party believed that localised government was most conducive to maintaining the dignity and autonomy of individuals. Support for Australia's federal system naturally accorded with the emphasis of Menzies and his Party on the individual, the family and the enterprises of the local community. The Liberal Party's support for federalism in its platform and policies distinguished it from the centralist tendencies of the ALP. As Australia's population grew considerably during the post-war years, Menzies' position was that the States would continue to exist and to attract considerable political support. Indeed the political clout of the States was often brought home to Menzies in his dealings with formidable premiers from both sides of politics during his prime ministership.

With the Menzies post-war government committed to national development, Menzies appreciated, however, that a critical new role for the Commonwealth was needed in leading a coordinated national approach to the domestic policies of infrastructural development, social welfare, healthcare and the growth of higher education. While Menzies spoke in favour of retaining a significant degree of autonomy for the States, his policies made the States increasingly dependent on Commonwealth grants with conditions attached.[16] Menzies embarked on new avenues of Commonwealth spending that were previously the prerogative of State governments, either exclusively or in conjunction with the Federal government. Such new spending initiatives included scholarships for university students; science laboratories in private schools and the rollout of private health insurance to supersede the provisions offered under the *Pharmaceuticals Benefits Act*. In addition, the Menzies government increased Commonwealth grants to the States which meant that the proportion of State fiscal resources derived from Federal funding increased from 41% in the 1949 budget to 54% in the 1964 budget.

With his government enlarging the responsibilities of the Commonwealth, it was Menzies' approach that rather than wholly taking over from the States in policy areas such as health and education, the Commonwealth would work in partnership with State governments to deliver services. Thus during his time as prime minister, the Commonwealth engaged more closely with the States in various fields of service delivery, particularly in the provision and operation of schools, hospitals, law enforcement, justice and correctional services, national parks, environmental management, personal welfare assistance, the regulation of workplaces and retail trade, electricity, ports, the support of mineral exploration, roads, water supply, housing and migrant hostels. According to JJ Pincus, 'Menzies was a pragmatic, centralising federalist, who generally welcomed the extensions of central powers and made use of them', but would do so always with the consent and cooperation of the States.

"So long as powers of government are divided between a central parliament, state parliament, municipal parliament...so long will there be no threat of tyranny because all those three powers won't be in the one hand. By dividing power you give yourself a protection against the concentration of power in one hand. And it's only by concentrating power in one hand that you get either fascism or communism or any other form of dictatorship of which these are merely variants"

Robert Menzies, Address to Apex Club Luncheon, Hotel Terrigal, 19 April 1958

"If the time comes when the Commonwealth is the sole provider of money, then make no mistake, the Commonwealth will have an unanswerable claim to be the sole holder of power because you can't separate power from responsibility without producing either tyranny on the one hand or anarchy on the other"

Robert Menzies, Address to Apex Club Luncheon, Hotel Terrigal, 19 April 1958

"Nationhood means a sense of common destiny. What is good for any part of Australia is good for the whole...I confess to being occasionally disappointed to find that we still think too much of

ourselves as citizens of a State and not sufficiently of ourselves as citizens of the nation"

Robert Menzies, 'Australia Today – Man to Man', Broadcast, 23 April 1958

"Most of us would feel that it would be a grave mistake to concentrate power in Canberra. State governments and local governments are physically near to the people with whom they deal, and the local problems with which they deal are in their nature not appropriate for remote control"

Robert Menzies, 'Australia Today – Man to Man', Broadcast, 30 April 1958

"The division of powers and responsibilities between the central and local parliaments has great merits. It would be a pity if, by not thinking about what we are doing, we drifted into a complete centralisation of power and gave Federation away"

Robert Menzies, 'Australia Today – Man to Man', Broadcast, 30 April 1958

"In common with very many other Australians I believe in Federalism; in the division of powers between central and local government; because I believe that in the long run the concentration of power in one set of hands is the enemy of individual freedom, but the division of power among several authorities is the most effective guarantee of individual freedom"

Robert Menzies, Support of the Liberal Party at the NSW State Elections, Broadcast, 20 February 1956

"State governments go on talking about being Sovereign States – that, of course, is not true. They exercise some Sovereign powers and the Commonwealth exercises some sovereign powers. The total of sovereignty resided in the community as a whole, and to talk about six Sovereign States is at once to assert that there is not a Sovereign Commonwealth. But, if we are to be a nation in the fullest sense, it will continue to be the fact that the most important factors in the life of the nation will be dealt with by the Commonwealth Parliament and by the Commonwealth Government"

Robert Menzies, Meeting of the Federal Executive of the

Liberal Party of Australia, Canberra, 6 April 1959

"All local prides and effort are admirable. That is why, in a great country like Australia, we have a federal system. But I repeat that the prime object of bringing about Federation in Australia was to create a nation"

Robert Menzies, The Challenge to Federalism, The University of Melbourne, 16 September 1960

"I believe that the future of this country, just like the future of any other democratic country, is largely associated with creating the national capital as a focus of interest, as a focus of pride, as a place which will attract the best possible men and women, not only for Parliament, for the Public Service, but for all the activities that are associated with Government on the grand scale. So I believe that all the investments that we are making in Canberra are dividend-paying investments in the best sense of the word"

Robert Menzies, Speech at the Opening of the Russell Offices, Canberra, 17 November 1960

"I am, myself, a Federalist. I don't wish to see unification in Australia. I don't wish to see all powers concentrated in Canberra. I think that the functions of the States are of great importance and that the division of power under a Federal system has a considerable relevance to the preservation of individual liberties in the community"

Robert Menzies, Inaugural John Storey Memorial Lecture, Melbourne, 8 December 1962

"What is good for Canberra, what makes this capital city a more lovely and attractive city, what enables this city to have directed to it the attention of millions of Australians is very good not only for Canberra but for Australia"

Robert Menzies, Inauguration of Lake Burley Griffin, 17 October 1964

"We have a natural instinct, haven't we in this country of ours, for parochialism for thinking in terms of states and of state loyalties, now these are admirable things, but the nation is the great element

in Australia. It's a hard and constant battle to make people understand that the Commonwealth is not a foreign power, that the Commonwealth is something that is interwoven through the whole structure of Australia and through the hearts and lives of all the people"

Robert Menzies, Inauguration of Lake Burley Griffin, 17 October 1964

"There is a pride in Canberra being developed...this is a matter of national importance, because more and more as people understand that this is the capital of the nation, a capital of which they may be proud, then more and more will they begin to realise instinctively that the nation is more important than any part of it"

Robert Menzies, Inauguration of Lake Burley Griffin, 17 October 1964

"I am, particularly for a large continent with widely scattered communities with great regional or local problems and understandable local prides and patriotisms, a Federalist. At our present stage of development, and for a long time to come, State Parliaments and Governments are and will be essential. The Constitution itself contemplates their continued existence and respects the powers 'reserved' for them"

Robert Menzies, 'Constitutional structure and the amending power', Lecture, University of Virginia, 10 October 1966

"I am a Federalist myself. I believe as I am sure most of you do, that in the division of powers between a Central Government and the State governments, there resides one of the true protections of individual freedom"

Robert Menzies, Central Power in the Australian Commonwealth: an examination of the growth of Commonwealth power in the Australian federation, London, 1967, p 24.

19

Social Welfare

On the occasion of his death in May 1978, the then leader of the NSW Liberals, Peter Coleman, remarked that Menzies had 'combined individualistic liberalism with a commitment to social welfare'.[17] As Prime Minister, Menzies consistently affirmed the need for Australia to maintain social security but always against the backdrop of liberal principles. Menzies' strategy of maximising individual initiative and free enterprise on the one hand, with the provision of ameliorative social welfare measures on the other, accorded with the thinking of key twentieth-century liberal theorists such as Friedrich Hayek. In *The Road to Serfdom* (1944), Hayek maintained that 'there is no incompatibility in principle between the state providing greater [social] security in this way and the preservation of individual freedom'.[18] Menzies affirmed this formula when he reflected that a modern state had much to gain from blending the ideals of rugged individualism with those of social responsibility. Repudiating the old *laissez-faire* strain of liberalism, Menzies was all too conscious that a free-enterprise economy devoid of any social security relief 'would tend to destroy the weak, impoverish the poor and reduce the dignity of the individual'.[19] For this reason, he believed governments had a social responsibility to provide a welfare safety net so long as it did not stultify individual initiative and perpetuate a culture of chronic welfare dependency.

After the defeat of the Chifley Labor government in December 1949, the Menzies government played an active role in maintaining and, indeed, extending social welfare by identifying new areas of need amongst the electorate. Social welfare policies under Menzies, however, would be designed to nurture and reward a constituency of 'lifters not leaners'.[20] In this vein, Menzies recalibrated welfare in terms of autonomy and self-reliance, placing free enterprise, volunteerism and the family at the heart of this reconceptualisation. Guided by the classic proverb, 'Give a man a fish and you feed him for a day; teach a man to fish and you feed him for a lifetime', Menzies and his government instinctively turned to job creation as the infinitely superior alternative to welfare dependency. As Henry Ergas and Jonathan Pincus appreciated, the goals of Menzies' social welfare policy were primarily pursued 'by an emphasis on job creation rather than through transfers'.[21] While mindful that welfare payments were often necessary to ameliorate short-term hardship, it was the provision of sustainable employment that ultimately enabled poorer individuals to not only earn a living for themselves but to become esteemed and productive members of society. For families meanwhile, the Menzies government in 1950 extended its original 1941 scheme of child endowment to the first (or only) child. Increases in the rates of endowment were intended to diminish poverty among large families, whilst student children between 16 and 21 became eligible to receive benefits under the scheme in 1964.[22] In addition to recipients of child endowment, individuals on various pension payments received increases in assistance during the Menzies era. Payment rates for age, invalid and widows' pensions were frequently adjusted upwards and, since the 1950s, they had increased more rapidly than living costs generally.[23]

As well as child endowment and pensions, the Menzies government introduced a suite of new social welfare initiatives including the free medicines service for pensioners, the 1954 Aged Persons' Homes Assistance scheme, the free provision of life-saving drugs, the provision of free milk for primary school children, the provision of special allowances as part of an attack on TB, rehabilitation allowances, the introduction of a Home Savings Grants Scheme in 1964 for young home buyers, and a substantial system of tax incentives and rewards.[23] In retrospect,

Menzies regarded such areas as health, pensions and benefits, aged care and housing as being among the 'high spots' of his record.[25]   With this commitment to social welfare, Menzies had put into practice his view, stated in his *Forgotten People* speech and often restated, that it was the responsibility of the state 'to secure, through social legislation, a decent and reasonable measure of economic security and material well-being for all responsible citizens'.[26]   In his implementation of social welfare policy as Prime Minister from 1949 to 1966, Menzies was assisted by a number of Ministers for Social Services including William Spooner (1949-51), Athol Townley (1951-54), William McMahon (1954-56), Hugh Roberton (1956-1965), and Ian Sinclair (1965-66).

While Menzies invested considerably in a welfare safety-net for individuals in need, the chief preoccupations of his government were to enlarge educational opportunities and generate job creation through the flourishing of free enterprise. Menzies appreciated that education and employment were the means through which individuals could develop into self-reliant contributors to society.   Returning to the theme of welfare dependency in 1964, Menzies concluded that during his prime ministership, the Australian electorate had come to repudiate the old socialist dependence on the state. He had observed, on the other hand, the emergence of:

> ...a younger and, on the whole, better educated generation of electors, who want the opportunity to make their own way and place in the world. They reject the enfeebling notion that the chief end of man, from the cradle to the grave, is to be ordered around by, and live dependent upon 'the government'.[26]

For Menzies, however, this did not justify a wholesale rejection of state intervention and return to *laissez-faire* but rather a just and prudent Government approach to social welfare that still allowed ample room for the blossoming of individual initiative and free enterprise. The chief end of social welfare policy for Menzies was never just about the economic empowerment of individuals but the advancement of their human dignity. Accordingly, his government favoured decidedly humane and personalised approaches to social welfare that best accorded with the material, social and spiritual needs of vulnerable persons such as the aged and those with a disability. For Menzies, the great priority of social welfare policy was the maximisation of what John Howard would later term the 'human dividend'.

"That we must do far more than in the past to give decent people some security in the face of sickness and unemployment is of course true. But in my opinion we must to the greatest possible extent do it upon the principle of contribution".

Robert Menzies, Opening Speech, Camberwell Town Hall, 23 July 1943

"Unemployment allowances or sickness allowances or medical provisions should where possible not be made on any basis which to the slightest degree smacks of charity. A worker who falls out of employment should be able to collect his unemployment insurance not as if he were going 'on the dole', but with self-respect as a man who collects something which is his right and to which in his days of employment he has made a contribution."

Robert Menzies, Opening Speech, Camberwell Town Hall, 23 July 1943

"Concentration upon Government action and the payment of social benefits entirely out of the public Treasury means the discouragement of thrift. Without thrift there can be no independence and without independent citizens there can be no independent nation…Thrift and independence must therefore be positively encouraged by our political policies. This involves a complete overhaul of our taxation system in order to help people with family responsibilities. It involves the conversion and extension of our social services on a contributory basis"

Robert Menzies, Opening Speech, Canberra Conference, 13 October 1944

"The Liberal Party stands unhesitatingly for the most ample provision in respect of old age and sickness and unemployment and widowhood and all the other economic and social misfortunes to which people are subject. But it says without equivocation that if all these things are to be provided on a sound, solvent and self-respecting basis they must be put upon a contributory footing"

Robert Menzies, Freemantle By-election, 15 August 1945

The Community has an obligation to give citizens a reasonable protection against misfortune. There must therefore be adequate provisions for old age, unemployment, invalidity, sickness and widowhood. The Liberal Party says all these things should be provided for out of the general revenue of the country, i.e., from the Treasury."

Robert Menzies, Social Services, Freemantle By-election, 15 August 1945

"A system of social services which depends upon community benevolence is inconsistent with the true basis of democracy – which includes the notion that social benefits should go to citizens as a right."

Robert Menzies, Social Services, Freemantle By-election, 15 August 1945

"We believe in fuller and better lives for every citizen; in better houses and schools and furniture and food and clothing, because it is in these things and not in mere terms of money that the real standard of living is to be found"

Robert Menzies, Provisional Policy Statement, 31 August 1945

"The purpose of all measures of social security is not only to provide citizens with some reasonable protection against misfortune but also to reconcile that provision with their proud independence and dignity as democratic citizens"

Robert Menzies, Provisional Policy Statement, 31 August 1945

"We Liberals believe that the first duty of the individual is a social duty. We believe that private business must, as a condition of its existence, observe liberal and humane industrial and social standards. We believe that we must have an adequate system of payments for old age, incapacity, sickness, medical expenses, unemployment, widowhood, and family endowment"

Robert Menzies, Election Speech, 20 August 1946

"The protection of the poor and the weak, and the elimination of the causes of poverty and weakness are undoubtedly the supreme business of politics. One can recognise that without in any way ceasing to insist that the first duty of every man is to do his utmost to stand on his own feet, to form his own judgments, and to accept his own responsibilities"

Robert Menzies, The First William Queale Memorial Lecture, Adelaide, 22 October 1954

"You will never have a government department of loving-kindness... you can't take loving-kindness up and put it in an Act of Parliament, you can't have a permanent head of the Department of Loving-kindness, you can't get people to fill in forms so that they may receive their due issue of loving-kindness. All these things can be done for a pension, for a benefit, for something, because those are matters that an enlightened public sense in the community requires that parliaments and governments should provide and of course they have to be organised, of course they must have all their rules"

Robert Menzies, Farewell to Dr Rayward, Sydney, 30 March, 1958

"Governments can only properly spend what individuals produce and earn. Our own tremendous increases in social services have been made possible only by our successful emphasis upon the encouragement of effort, and skill, and production, and the building up of a virile population, possessed of initiative and enterprise"

Robert Menzies, General Elections 1958, Broadcast, 19 November 1958

"An uncontrolled and unregulated free competitive enterprise would tend to destroy the weak, impoverish the poor, and reduce that dignity of the individual man and woman which it must be the purpose of democracy to create and enhance"

Robert Menzies, First Baillieu Lecture, 6 July 1964

"The great social problem of our times, the great social problem of the last ten years, fifteen years, has been to create in our social services an abiding and warm sense of humanity not of charity, but of loving kindness in the true sense, of friendliness. So that everybody, whether he's living or she's living in a great mansion on inherited riches or living here or living somewhere else, will feel that there is an atmosphere of human kindness and that we, the people of Australia, are not being charitable or condescending, but that we are friends together."

Robert Menzies, Opening of the Vasey Housing Auxiliary Homes at Manningtree Road, Hawthorn, Victoria, 17 March, 1963

"We have greatly aided social justice. We have not just kept the ring and allowed victory to go to the strong. We have encouraged free enterprise, have recognised the making of a people as one of the dynamic inducements to the taking of capital risks in the development of the nation. But we have insisted upon the performance of social and industrial obligations; we have shown that industrial progress is not to be based upon the poverty or despair of those who cannot compete."

Robert Menzies, Speech to the Federal Council of the Liberal Party, Canberra, 6 April 1964

20

Socialism and Communism

As Prime Minister during the Cold War, Menzies is often remembered as much for his anti-Communism as for his pro-British sentiment. His ill-fated attempt in 1951 to ban the Communist Party of Australia under the Constitution and his policy of Forward Defence to contain Communism in South East Asia were of course well known, but what did Menzies actually have to say about Communism itself and why was this ideology so distasteful to his own instincts and philosophy? Indeed the liberal creed of Menzies could be defined almost as much by the ideals it stood for, namely, free enterprise, individual liberties and the rule of law, as much as the traits it stood against such as social division, centralised authority and Socialism. In the context of the Cold War, Menzies accepted that the tradition of political liberalism, even within Australia, was far from unassailable and required a rigorous apologetic to refute the claims of Communism and socialism. While the organised Communist movement itself in Australia was numerically small with no real prospect of seizing power, its doctrine of Socialism did hold sway within the Labour movement, albeit in the much milder form of democratic socialism. To be sure, the Labor Party of Chifley expressly repudiated the authoritarian Communism of regimes such as the Soviet Union but its 'socialist objective' to socialise 'industry, production, distribution and exchange' troubled Menzies. Accordingly a robust liberal movement was needed to counter both the advance of Socialism in domestic politics and the threat of Communism from abroad.

In *Afternoon Light*, Menzies reflected that he had never 'been attracted by State Socialism', even as an idealistic young student. 'From my earliest days until now', wrote Menzies, 'I have found Socialism a dreary and essentially reactionary doctrine'. He was broadminded enough, however, to understand the historic appeal of socialism in an age where unregulated market forces had produced enormous economic equality, where the unscrupulous captains of industry were free to exploit masses of vulnerable workers including children, where Trade Unionism was virtually non-existent and where no welfare safety-net existed to protect families incurring financial hardship. Menzies appreciated that these social and economic maladies had driven many citizens of goodwill to support the Labor movement but remained resolutely unconvinced that the creed of socialism could provide the right remedies. For Menzies, the solution lay not in the socialist prescription for enforced uniformity and bigger government, but in the revival of a civilised capitalism which affirmed the rights and obligations of individuals in society.

Menzies' philosophical objection to socialism and communism arose from his belief that these conformist ideologies were fundamentally incompatible with human nature and therefore detrimental to human flourishing. For Menzies and other liberals, human beings were purposely created as *individuals* with differing personalities, dispositions, talents and energies. As such, people would be drawn to different vocations where there would again be apparent variations in approach, method, style, pace and work output. Indeed the very progress of society was dependent upon the diversity of its citizens and their personal freedom to exercise judgment and choice. While Menzies affirmed the equality of opportunity for all citizens 'to strive, to seek, to find and not to yield', the equality of outcome favoured by socialism would prove elusive as individual men and women failed to conform to a uniform pattern of performance prescribed by the state. Menzies simply saw the rigid prism of State Socialism as incapable of providing for the diversity of schools, colleges, enterprises and associations that afforded each and every individual the freedom to choose, the freedom to flourish and the freedom to simply be oneself.

In their suppression of human individuality, particularly in the realms of education and employment, socialism and communism represented the enemies of free enterprise. Under a socialist regime, Menzies feared that the State's monopoly over industry and enterprise would serve to destroy, or at the very least frustrate, the capacity for private companies, businesses and family-owned firms to build the country and contribute to the national economy. As Menzies campaigned to lead his Liberal party to government in the late 1940s, he expressed concern that the Chifley Labor government was giving the State too much control over industry and enterprise, particularly with its bank nationalisation policy. As one of the most socialist measures taken by an Australian government to date, Menzies strenuously opposed the Chifley government's 1947 bill to nationalise the banks because it would suppress the 'normal liberty of choice' for citizens to choose their own bank and further entrench the notion of government supremacy. Upon his election as Prime Minister in 1949, Menzies accordingly sought to arrest this post-war trend towards socialised industry to 'instead seek the private enterprise answer'. For Menzies, it was not just government departments but also the 'forgotten people' of small business owners, shopkeepers, skilled artisans, professionals and farmers who were the great generators of enterprise and jobs in the nation. As important as public sector agencies would remain for the provision of employment opportunities, they needed to be supplemented by a robust and flourishing private sector that could afford job security and acceptable living standards for individual Australians. Menzies maintained that 'in its objective of providing better living standards and security for all, the State will be greatly aided by a vigorous, healthy and enlightened private enterprise'.[28]

The menace of socialism and communism for Menzies, however, was not simply social and economic but also moral and spiritual. The worldview of Communism, especially, was deficient because its narrow, materialistic thesis of class warfare failed to appreciate the essential, spiritual impulses of the human heart. Menzies conceived of these spiritual instincts in Christian terms where human beings under the fatherhood of

God were called to the 'obligations of mutual love and understanding' as brothers and sisters. Denouncing communism as not only illiberal but also 'pagan', Menzies argued that its social doctrine of class envy and conflict ran directly counter to Christian principles. In his 1951 election campaign speech, he said that Communism 'derives from the darkest recesses of the human mind' and 'has nothing in common with the Christian gospel of love and brotherhood'. According to Menzies, Communism's fostering of hatred between people was 'no instrument of progress but [was] merely a sign of decadence and despair'. With Communism's antipathy towards Christian values, it had suppressed the religious freedom of Christians and people of other faiths in the Soviet Union and Communist-controlled regions of East Asia. Indeed, with its repression of all religious freedom, Menzies regarded the 'spiritual slavery' of Communism as 'much worse' than its physical slavery.

For Menzies, socialism and communism were not only destructive to economic, personal and religious liberty but also to national unity. With socialism and communism, to varying degrees, drawing upon Karl Marx's theory of class struggle between the bourgeois and proletariat, Menzies deplored the attempts of socialists to inflame class tensions. In his *Forgotten People* Address, Menzies denounced class warfare as a 'false war' and as Australia's 'greatest political disease'. Rejecting the Socialist premise that the interests of employers and employees under capitalism were fundamentally opposed, Menzies and his Liberal party instead affirmed that the interests of workers and their managers were complementary. Each needed the other to succeed and mutual cooperation rather than conflict was deemed critical to driving progress and prosperity. Whereas Marxism preached conflict, envy and division between the working-class and middle-class, an authentic liberalism promoted class harmony and cooperation. Indeed for Menzies, the only 'great and honourable class distinction in Australia was that between the industrious and the idle' which rendered the whole Marxist notion of a class struggle meaningless and out of date. Whether a citizen was a blue-collar worker or a white-collar worker, they each shared a stake in the prosperity and welfare of the country. Rejecting the socialist politics of division, liberalism's doctrine of complementarity between working-class and middle-class, employer and employee provided the formula for national unity and progress.

"Any government that seeks to put the dead hand of socialism on Australia will produce in this country a flabby community lacking in backbone, lacking in spirit and initiative, that will go down the river in the first flood"

Robert Menzies, The Individual in the New Order, City Hall, Brisbane, 21 January 1943

"What is the essence of Communism? If those who established it knew anything about it, we must assume that Communism is a political and social doctrine of violence and conflict, of the class war leading to the dictatorship of the proletariat. It is founded upon the belief that the conflict must be carried on if necessary, and indeed probably, with arms and bloodshed, and that as a result of a great clash of hatreds and of wills, we will ultimately emerge into a classless society in which all men will be equal in the eyes of an all-powerful State. Its thesis is entirely material"

Robert Menzies, The Communists, Broadcast, 2 July 1943

"Show me a Nation in which everybody lives on the government and I will unhesitatingly declare it a nation whose decline and fall are at hand."

Robert Menzies, Opening Speech, Camberwell Town Hall, 23 July 1943

"Christianity on the other hand sets out an entirely different philosophy. It denies the inevitable mutual hostility of social groups; it preaches the obligations of mutual understanding and love; it does not see the progress of men as something produced by the class war, by the violent clash of economic interests, by the surging to and fro of purely material movements. It calls on human beings to love their enemies and to do good to those who misuse them. It subordinates the purely material factors of life to the spiritual factors. It seeks to make men understand that there

will never be a brotherhood of man over all the world except by the acknowledgement of a common Fatherhood"

Robert Menzies, The Communists, Broadcast, 2 July 1943

"Of all the world's systems of government that of a liberal democracy is the best because it alone recognises the infinite variations of human nature and the unlimited potentialities of the individual human being. Communism in this country is the enemy of these things. It is illiberal, pagan, violent, and essentially dictatorial. It does not believe in parliament. It does not believe in cooperation or understanding. It does not believe in the country that shelters it and that has given it the privilege of shouting its garbled nonsense from the street corner and through the wireless microphone"

Robert Menzies, The Communists, Broadcast, 2 July 1943

"I see the individual and his encouragement and recognition as the prime motive force for the building of a better world. Socialism means high costs, inefficiency, the constant intrusion of political considerations, the damping down of enterprise, the overlordship of routine. None of these elements can produce progress, and without progress, security will turn out to be a delusion"

Robert Menzies, Forming the Liberal Party of Australia, Record of the Conference of Representatives of Non-Labour Organisations, Canberra, 13-14 October, 1944

"The Labour Party sees the way to human happiness through more and more government action and control all round. Wherever some problem crops up, the Labour Socialist's immediate reaction is to pass another law, create another department, enlist another army of government servants, proclaim another set of regulations containing more rules and restrictions, and give us another set of forms to fill in"

Robert Menzies, The Choice, Broadcast, 1946

"For there can be no real freedom in a community in which the government controls our employment, and directs our lives, and runs the newspapers and the broadcasting stations, and tells us when we shall work, and how."

Robert Menzies, The Choice, Broadcast, 1946

"The modern socialist is so obsessed with his belief that the State is the best employer and should be the only one, and that the ills of mankind can be dealt with either medically or surgically by legislation, that his automatic response to a problem is to devise a new law and create a new department"

Robert Menzies, Freedom and the Call to Action, Lecture to Junior Chamber of Commerce, 4 August 1947

"If there is to grow up in perpetuity in Australia this miserable sense of dependence upon the State, then the only question that will arise will be whether we are first swallowed by a Fascist dictatorship at home or by aggressive and virile enemies from without"

Robert Menzies, Socialised Banking: Instrument of Tyranny, Speech at Sydney Town Hall, 25 August 1947

"If freedom connotes the full use of the powers that God has given man, than there can be no freedom in the all-powerful State or in the servile mass mind"

Robert Menzies, 'Bond or Free', Wesley Church, Melbourne, 7 September 1947

"This bill goes far beyond banking. It will have an operation and effect far beyond the business of money changing. This bill will be a tremendous step towards the servile State, because it will set aside normal liberty of choice and that is what competition means, and will forward the idea of the special supremacy of government. That is the antithesis of democracy."

Robert Menzies, The Banking Bill (1947), Second Reading Speech, House of Representatives, 23 October 1947

"Wherever dictatorship exists it is obvious that it would be forwarded very much more by a single politically-established monopoly bank than by all the competing banks operating separately"

Robert Menzies, The Banking Bill (1947), Second Reading Speech, House of Representatives, 23 October 1947

"Are we for the Socialist State, with its subordination of the individual to the universal officialdom of government, or are we for the ancient British faith that governments are the servants of the people, a faith

which has given fire and quality and direction to the whole of our history for 600 years?"

Robert Menzies, Election Speech, 10 November 1949

"Communism is a materialistic doctrine, void of spiritual content. It is not only anti-Christian, but is opposed to all those nobler aspirations which spring from the religious faith of decent people."

Robert Menzies, Election Speech, March 1951

"We must, before we cast down our defences, be warned against the woolly-minded thinking which regards Communism as just another religion to be respected and tolerated; and Communist nations as just friendly but misunderstood neighbours. I say to people who think this way, and I say it with all the spirit of my Scottish ancestors, that there can be no compromise between Christ and the anti-Christ, between the cynical and merciless doctrines and practices of imperialist Communism and the old, yet new, evangel of the Sermon on the Mount"

Robert Menzies, General Elections 1955: Defence, Broadcast, 17 November 1955

"We have no hostility in our minds except to communism and it is our dearest hope that there may arise true democracies, informed by self-government and devoted to peace, who will stand against communist aggression and will give us friends and neighbours with whom we may live at peace and with mutual understanding"

Robert Menzies, General Elections 1958, Broadcast, 10 November 1958

"Communism is to be resisted not only by force of arms, though we must not shrink from that. It is also to be resisted by the developed character of people, by the building up of their own genuine belief in their own freedom, by the improvement in their own economy. It is to be resisted, as I said last year at a Council Meeting in Washington, by developing a sense of community which will translate the South-East Asia Treaty Organisation into a genuine community of self-interest, of self-reliance, and of mutual trust"

Robert Menzies, Statement at SEATO, 27 March 1961

"Don't let us succumb to the idea that the great conflict in the world is a conflict between the power of the United States, for example, and the power of the Soviet Union. This is a false picture. The conflict in the world is a conflict between basic principles, profoundly important ideals, differences of outlook on the spirit of man, and the significance of man; a conflict, as we would wish to believe, between what, from our point of view, is the Christian conception of the freedom of the human mind and of the human spirit, and the dictated, dominated, unfree human spirit that exists under totalitarian Government in the Communist regime"

Robert Menzies, 'Pleasant Sunday Afternoon', Melbourne, 3 September 1961

"We must remember all the time that while physical slavery is a terrible thing, spiritual slavery is much worse"

Robert Menzies, 'Pleasant Sunday Afternoon', Melbourne, 3 September 1961

"Whenever I hear the Communists or near Communists talking about the class struggle so much beloved of Marx, I remind myself that in this country of mine and yours, all that class stuff is out of date. You're a worker or you're not"

Robert Menzies, Young Liberals Rally, Hawthorn, 6 July 1962

"As I have many times said, Socialism is both reactionary and out-dated. I can understand how it attracted the support of radical thinkers after the industrial revolution in Great Britain and later at the turn of the century, when industrial power was in a limited number of hands, when the rights of employed people were imperfectly recognised, when trades unions were too commonly regarded as subversive bodies, when the economic doctrines of laissez-faire held sway, when social services were almost non-existent, there grew up in many minds a belief an egalitarian belief in the virtues of uniformity"

Robert Menzies, Speech to the Federal Council of the Liberal Party, Canberra, 6 April 1964

21

War and Peace

Serving as Prime Minister through both the early phase of the Second World War and the Cold War, the spectre of war was never far from Menzies' mind. Although Menzies did not serve in uniform during the Great War of his youth, he was not oblivious to the indelible scars its carnage had left on hundreds and thousands of families and communities throughout Australia. With Menzies believing up until the late 1930s that the Great War had been 'the war to end all wars', he shared the aversion of his fellow Australians to the prospect of yet another global conflagration. For this reason, Menzies supported Neville Chamberlain of Britain with his cautious policy of appeasement towards Nazi Germany. Writing to Chamberlain in August 1939, he wrote that 'No nation should ignore real efforts at settlement because of false notions of prestige' and deplored war as 'the greatest possible calamity'. While Menzies was no pacifist, he was nonetheless convinced that the negotiation of a binding peace-settlement with Hitler would be infinitely preferable to a declaration of war on Nazi Germany. In his approach to the Nazi question, Menzies largely continued the policy of his UAP predecessor Joe Lyons but distanced himself from the more hawkish outlook of Chamberlain's successor, Winston Churchill, in the late 1930s. Destructive, barbarous and uncivilised, war to Menzies represented a 'failure of the human spirit' and was a fate to be averted at all costs.

With Britain's declaration of war on 3 September 1939, however, Menzies immediately 'declared that Australia was also at war'. From the tone of his broadcast, it was evident that Menzies dreaded this outbreak of war but owing to both Australia's loyalty to Britain and its international obligations to defend other European nations from Nazi German belligerence, he determined that it was right to involve Australia. As a wartime Prime Minister, Menzies and his government prepared Australia for war by announcing the commitment of troops to join British forces and undertook administrative reforms to increase the capacity of Australia's defence departments. Eager to lead a united political front during the War, Menzies invited Labor to join his UAP in forming a national government, but the ALP rebuffed the offer. Appreciating the critical role of Britain in the execution of the war, Menzies travelled to Britain in early 1941 to hold talks with Churchill and his War Cabinet. Despite some historical perceptions that Menzies simply jettisoned Australia's interests in the Pacific to curry favour with Churchill, the Australian Prime Minister protested at his British counterpart's inability to understand the situation in Singapore or the vulnerability of Britain's dominions in the Pacific.[29] As well as defending Australia's interests abroad, Menzies made overtures to Ireland and Canada to enlist their support for the British war effort, but was unsuccessful. Shortly after his return to Australia in May 1941, the support of his UAP colleagues crumbled and Menzies relinquished the Prime Ministership on 28 August.

Whilst no longer Prime Minister, Menzies continued to take an abiding interest in the war, indeed his very decision to resign was motivated principally by wartime considerations. With Australia at war, Menzies believed that national unity was paramount and given his contentious position within the UAP, he saw his decision to resign as 'offering real prospects of unity in the ranks of the government party'. A destabilised and divided government, on the other hand, would serve only to cripple the morale and leadership the country desperately needed to see the crisis through. Menzies used his time in the political wilderness to broadcast regular messages to the people and many of these 1942 addresses frequently alluded to the then omnipresent theme of war and peace. Menzies spoke about how the war represented not only a clash of national interests but the struggle for the survival of democracy in the face of tyranny. Turning to specific themes, Menzies spoke on 'women in war', 'the schools in war', 'the moral element in total war' and 'paying for the war'. With his eyes fixed on the future, Menzies also spoke presciently about the shape of affairs following the war. In 1942, he hoped for a world where both the Germans and Japanese could 'live and move in amity with ourselves', a vision which soon came to pass as the former axis powers each emerged as a constructive contributor to the peace and prosperity of the post-war world. While Menzies had argued in 1942 that the nation required its immediate energy and resources for a sustained war effort to overcome the enemy; the resumption of peace, in his poetic phrase, would require the people to once again 'beat their swords into ploughshares'. Accordingly, industry, agriculture, development and education would be charged with the task of rebuilding the country after the war.

Menzies viewed peace in a very similar vein to that of freedom, like the notion of liberty itself, he saw peace as ultimately springing from the character of individual nations and their people. Accordingly, his faith in the capacity of the United Nations to guarantee world peace was somewhat more circumspect than that of his Labor opponents such as H V Evatt. While Menzies envisaged a legitimate role for the UN, he believed that alliances and bilateral relations between freedom-loving nations such as Australia, New Zealand, Britain and the US proved the best means of securing peace. The best way to advance world peace was not simply to build a stronger UN with more binding declarations and covenants on its member nations, but rather the cultivation of peace-loving ideals, such as freedom, tolerance and justice, across the nations of the world. In just the same way that the State could not enforce democracy on its own citizens, it was naïve to believe that an international organ such as the UN could impose peace on its member states, particularly those bereft of intrinsic peace-loving principles. The proper pathway to lasting peace, therefore, was for nations such as Australia to stand in solidarity with other free nations, and together, they could forge constructive trade relations with other countries which would then open up avenues to commend free, democratic ideals for these countries to adopt for themselves. Menzies held that the creation of constructive and fruitful trade relations between countries could lay a firm foundation for world peace.

"Fellow Australians, it is my melancholy duty to inform you officially that, in consequence of a persistence by Germany in her invasion of Poland, Great Britain has declared war upon her, and that, as a result, Australia is also at war. No harder task can fall to the lot of a democratic leader than to make such an announcement"

Robert Menzies, Declaration of War, Broadcast, 3 September 1939

"Bitter as we all feel at this wanton crime, this is not a moment for rhetoric; prompt as the action of many thousands must be, it is for the rest a moment for quiet thinking, for that calm fortitude which rests not upon the beating of drums, but upon the unconquerable spirit of man, created by God in His own image. What may be before us we do not know; nor how long the journey. But this we do know: That truth is our companion on that journey, that truth is with us in the battle, and that truth must win"

Robert Menzies, Declaration of War, Broadcast, 3 September 1939

"It is not by a treaty that we shall pass out of this hideous valley of death into the higher lands of peace and goodwill. Peace may be all sorts of things – a real end of war, a mere exhaustion, an armed interlude before the next struggle. But it will only be by a profound stirring in the hearts of men that we shall reach goodwill."

Robert Menzies, Hatred as an Instrument of War, 10 April 1942

"When this war is over we all hope to live in a better world in which both Germans and Japanese, violently purged of their lust for material power, will be able to live and move in amity with ourselves and in that friendly intercourse which is a more

powerful instrument of peace than any artificial plan ever devised"

Robert Menzies, Hatred as an Instrument of War, 10 April 1942

"War after war is the result of a failure of the human spirit, not of some superficial elements but of the fatal inability of man to adjust himself to other men in a social world"

Robert Menzies, Education, Parliamentary Debates, House of Representatives, 26 July 1945

"I have for many years believed that the best way of ensuring peace is not by resolutions of great assemblies but by the steady grouping together of genuinely peace-loving nations so that more and more areas may be established in which, as in the British Empire itself, as in the United States of America, there can be no thought of aggressive war or of any dispute incapable of being settled by reasons and the common principles of justice"

Robert Menzies, Broadcast for New Zealand, 26 January 1954

"The second World War was thought likely to usher in a new era of internationalism. It has, in fact, led to a new wave of acute nationalism, frequently marred by racial bitterness, and accompanied by a new Communist imperialism all the more sinister because it professes to be the foe of imperialism"

Robert Menzies, Address to the Tenth Session of the Australasian Medical Congress, Hobart, 5 March 1958

"Hitler is defeated and dead, but his harsh theories of racial superiority have left many converts. Mussolini is overthrown and dead, but his irredentist fancies are flourishing elsewhere"

Robert Menzies, Address to the Tenth Session of the Australasian Medical Congress, Hobart, 5 March 1958

"In my own lifetime, twice Australia has been involved in war, in enmity, but neither time because Australia wanted to be anybody's opponent, but because somebody wanted to be the opponent of Australia and what Australia believed in...we are a peaceful people. We are capable of being warlike for a time, but always with the ambition for peace"

Robert Menzies, Speech at Dinner Tendered by His Excellency, First Minister Djuanda of Indonesia, 2 December,

1959

"You can't establish peace in the world just by passing resolutions, or even by making disarmament agreements. You can establish peace only when you persuade the countries and peoples of the world that they live in a state of justice, that they have, each of them, a fair deal"

Robert Menzies, "Pleasant Sunday Afternoon", Melbourne, 4 September 1960

"I am old-fashioned enough to believe that the greatest guarantee of peace in the world is that nations should trade peacefully plentifully and profitably with each other. This is a tremendous foundation for understanding and therefore for peace"

Robert Menzies, Opening of the ANZ Bank Building, Pitt and Hunter Streets, Sydney, 24 September 1965

"In times of peace…the hardest thing is to project into contemporary affairs the spirit of comradeship and sacrifice and patriotism at its best that we have accommodated ourselves to in times of war. This is terribly difficult. Men who, under the great heat and pressure of events in a war will perform miracles of self-sacrifice, will not have that feeling at all in time of peace and yet, without being too grandiloquent about it, this is what we need"

Robert Menzies, Speech at Dover's Maison Dieu (Town Hall), 20 July 1966

"We are tempted to think that the defence of the realm is something which occurs in terms of arms and nothing else. Arms, war, the defence of the realm. But the defence of the realm is a continuing thing. The defence of the realm includes the defence of its, to be quite homely, its economic structure, its prosperity, its social justice, its institutions, the rule of parliamentary democracy, the rule of law, all of these things are matters which have to be defended. Don't take them for granted. They have been destroyed in many parts of the world overnight"

Robert Menzies, Speech at Dover's Maison Dieu (Town Hall), 20 July 1966

22

Women

In cultural perceptions of Australia in the 1950s, Menzies has loomed large as the champion of the male breadwinner/female homemaker nuclear family. As such, he is frequently regarded as a cultural relic who inhabited a pre-feminist world of male privilege and domination yet the evidence suggests Menzies entertained a keen interest in the advancement of women both inside and outside the Liberal Party. The founder of the Liberal Party was committed to empowering women within the institutional structure of his new party while also envisioning a post-war society where women would be emboldened to realise their full potential in any field of endeavour. The attitude of Menzies towards women entered the public record in the early 1940s and was informed by both his political philosophy of liberalism and his personal experiences of the Second World War.

Even before his first elevation to the prime ministership in 1939, Menzies had collaborated with like-minded women from the Victorian-based Australian Women's National League (AWNL), a liberal conservative group formed in 1903. Like Menzies himself, the anti-socialist AWNL was heavily influenced by the philosophy of English liberalism, with its belief in private enterprise and the independence of the individual, together with the tradition of Nonconformist Protestantism (particularly Methodism) which stressed the values of community service and domestic propriety. Whilst the AWNL had opposed women's suffrage in its early years, its leaders, including Elizabeth Couchman, were committed to recruiting more women into anti-Labor politics in the 1930s and 40s. Indeed Couchman herself became a close personal friend of Menzies and helped bring the AWNL into the fold of the Liberal Party in 1944, a development Menzies wholeheartedly welcomed. With the input of Couchman and the AWNL, the new Liberal Party made an unprecedented pitch to female voters with women addressed directly in advertising and in speeches. As Fitzherbert noted, the Party's campaign advertising and policy promotion materials were gender inclusive.

With the Liberal Party appealing to female voters, its founder and leader made no bones about his guiding belief in the inherent equality of men and women. In the tradition of the English liberal philosopher, John Stuart Mill, Menzies argued that there were no rational grounds for believing that women should be denied the same opportunities as men in society simply because of their sex. If men and women were equally endowed with various intellectual and athletic faculties, then there was no reason why women should be inhibited from exercising these to any lesser extent than men. Like Mill in *The Subjugation of Women* (1869), Menzies regarded existing impediments to women's participation in education, the professions and public life as a compromise to the liberal principle of individual freedom. It was only by giving women a free reign to cultivate their individual talents and realise their potential that societies such as Australia could enjoy greater freedom and social progress.

Critical to the formation of Menzies' own views on women was his experience of witnessing women serve at the coalface of the war effort in Australia and Britain. In the early 1940s, Menzies deeply admired the proficiency, stamina and resourcefulness of women who served as truck and ambulance drivers, land army corps, fire-fighters and factory workers. To him, this was vindication of his Mill-inspired liberal philosophy that women were eminently capable of exercising their skills and abilities when given the opportunity to do so. In a prescient observation of future trends, Menzies described 'this great movement of women into the defence of the realm' as a 'formidable breaking down of old barriers and old ideas'. He welcomed this as a progressive step which would see Australia benefit from the full contribution of its female citizens.

During and after the War, Menzies and his Party sought to lead by example in their resolve to encourage more women to seek political office. To be sure, progress towards increasing the participation of women was slow but there were some noteworthy breakthroughs. In the 1943 Federal election, the UAP's Enid Lyons became the first woman to be elected to the House of Representatives. After the formation of the Liberal Party in 1944, Annabelle Rankin of Queensland entered the Senate in 1947. In 1949, she was joined in the Senate by Ivy Wedgwood of Victoria and Agnes Robertson of Western Australia. Under Menzies, Enid Lyons became the first woman to be a member of Federal Cabinet, serving as Vice-President of the Executive Council in 1949. In 1951, Senator Rankin became the first woman to be party whip in the Federal Parliament and in 1955, Nancy Buttfield of South Australia added to the number of female Senators. With the entry of more women into parliament, the Menzies government enacted some policies that were targeted at women. These included the extension of child endowment to first-born children and the introduction of free milk for school children in 1950. In 1962, the Women's Bureau was created in the Department of Labour and National Service to investigate policy in relation to women in the paid workforce.

While Menzies actively encouraged the participation of women in politics as both party members and MPs, he proved to be a traditionalist with respect to the role of women within the domestic sphere. His government's system of tax deductions introduced in the early 1950s tended to favour families with a male breadwinner and stay-at-home mother.[30] When it came to changing the requirement that women retire from the public service on marriage, Menzies refused to remove the 'marriage bar' despite the urging by some of his female parliamentary colleagues to do so. Notwithstanding his conservative views on the role of women in the *family*, his attitudes towards the role of women in *society* were fairly progressive. In the 1950s, he declared that he had 'no inhibitions about women in careers', deeming 'competence' to be the sole criterion for determining a woman's success in her field of choice. In the realm of public life and international affairs, Menzies held that women had an equal stake to men and that the division between public and private life was non gender-specific. Although some modern feminists may regard Menzies' views on the role of women as somewhat contradictory, he saw his own views as eminently complementary, appreciating a healthy society to be reliant upon both the stability of family life and the personal freedom of women to contribute to professional and public life. In short, Menzies was committed to a feminism that was liberating and empowering but not socially disruptive.

"In the long run, won't the country be a stronger, better balanced and more intelligent community when the last artificial disabilities imposed upon women by centuries of custom have been removed? There is no equality so ennobling as an equality in sacrifice. There is perhaps nothing that we need more as a corrective to the patent ills of democracy than a full brotherhood and sisterhood in action and sacrifice"

Robert Menzies, Women in War, Broadcast, 20 February 1942

"Higher education for women must come to be regarded as normal and not as the eccentricity of a potential 'blue stocking'. For the blunt truth is that the equality of the sexes cannot be maintained if a slapdash training in a few minor ornamental accomplishments is considered an adequate education for the daughter of the house"

Robert Menzies, Schools and the War, Broadcast, 16 October 1942

"Of course women are at least the equals of men. Of course there is no reason why a qualified woman should not sit in parliament or on the bench or in professorial chair, or preach from the pulpit, or,

if you like, command an army in the field. No educated man today denies a place or career to a woman just because she is a woman"

Robert Menzies, Women for Canberra, Broadcast, 29 January 1943

"For myself, I decline to vote for any woman just because she is a woman...I am not half so interested in the sex or social position or world wealth of my representatives and rulers as I am in the quality of their minds, the soundness of their characters, the humanity of their experiences, the sanity of their policy, and the strength of their wills"

Robert Menzies, Women for Canberra, Broadcast, 29 January 1943

"We should shake our minds clear of whatever prejudice may linger in them and honestly and sincerely acknowledge that there is just as much room in all our public bodies for public-spirited and intelligent women as there is for public-spirited and intelligent men"

Robert Menzies, Women for Canberra, Broadcast, 29 January 1943

"Women are unquestionably destined to exercise more and more influence upon practical politics in Australia. There was a time when they were thought to stand aside, exercising only passive influence. That has gone. In the educating of the electorate in liberal ideas they have for many years been an effective force. Now we have an organisation in which all distinctions have gone, and with men and women working equally for the one body the resultant education value of our movement is going to be extremely increased'"

Robert Menzies, Speech at the Conclusion of the Albury Conference, 16 December 1944

"Tonight I speak to the women of Australia with profound respect and gratitude. They have established an unanswerable claim to economic, legal, industrial, and political equality. I hope that the time will speedily come when we can say truthfully that there is no sex discrimination in public or private office, in political or industrial opportunity. We are all, men and women, citizens with

a common interest and a common task"

Robert Menzies, Election Speech, 20 August 1946

"We have never accepted the view that men and women have an entirely distinct interest in politics, or that only some of its problems are for the consideration of women. The truth is that all the great questions of policy and administration affect men and women in equal degree"

Robert Menzies, Address to a public meeting of women, 11 November 1949

"I have frequently had to say to my female political friends, 'look, don't ask people to vote for you because you are a woman. Ask them to vote for you because you are the best man in the field. You are the one to represent them. You are the one who will understand public problems'"

Robert Menzies, Speech to the Conference of the Headmistresses' Association of Australia, Melbourne, 1 September, 1958

"The very great determining problems of politics, of international affairs, of high policy, of economics, of finance, of the things that barely put their hand out and touch the ordinary lives of people – these problems have no sex at all. They must be understood equally by men and women if they are to be dealt with in the parliament of the nation and in the government of the nation"

Robert Menzies, Speech to the Conference of the Headmistresses' Association of Australia, Melbourne, 1 September, 1958

"If women are to occupy themselves in careers in life, in any of the professions, in any of the great activities, then they will be the first to concede that in that field they must be able to stand on their own feet, in that field they must measure in competence against the people who are their rivals. I wouldn't like to have you believe for one moment that I have any inhibitions about women in careers"

Robert Menzies, Speech to the Conference of the Headmistresses' Association of Australia, Melbourne, 1 September, 1958

"There will increasingly be in the modern world, women of singular talent who will devote themselves to careers, not just because they want to earn a living but because they have something in them that they must express. So we will have, as we have had in the past, women of immense talents in various professions, and to them the whole world should be open"

Robert Menzies, Speech to the Conference of the Headmistresses' Association of Australia, Melbourne, 1 September, 1958

23

Wit and Humour

In an interview with the ABC in 2011, the daughter of Robert Menzies, Heather Henderson, reminded audiences that her father had a human side and an integral part of that was his sense of humour. The anecdotes of his daughter and other close relations suggest that Menzies exhibited this attribute in private company amongst family, friends and trusted colleagues, as well as in public appearances on the political stage. Indeed the key to Menzies' appeal as a statesman and success as a parliamentarian was his ability to combine a formal, stately demeanour with a penchant for cracking witticisms and comical 'one-liners'. The transcripts of Menzies' speeches are frequently punctuated by wry remarks, self-deprecating jibes, puns, whimsical jests and, of course, the quick-witted rejoinders for which he was famous. Like all good humourists, his humour displayed the verbal gymnastics of word-play, idiom and hyperbole to give colour and rhetorical effect to his message.

At testimonials, black-tie dinners, state receptions, school speech nights, university graduations and opening ceremonies for hospitals or factories, Menzies frequently used humour as a tool to amuse, entertain and enthral audiences. The comical moments in his speeches were very often extempore and not part of the prepared script which gave them all the more liveliness and authenticity. When asked whether he stuck to his prearranged text, he replied, 'Not quite. I do interlard prepared speeches with a few asides...I find it much better to have an audience laugh occasionally than sleep all the time'. Like a good preacher or lecturer, Menzies well understood the supreme effect a little humour had in piquing the attention of a weary audience. The addition of just a few jokes or witticisms could mean the difference between one's messages falling on live or deaf ears.

As well as its entertainment value, Menzies used humour as a weapon to wither his political opponents. One of his frequent sparring partners in the parliamentary chamber was Labor's Eddie Ward, the firebrand Member for East Sydney who once famously described Menzies as 'a posturing individual with the scowl of a Mussolini, the bombast of a Hitler and the physical proportions of a Göring'. When Ward once accused Menzies of displaying his superiority again, Menzies shot back, saying that 'there are times when one cannot help feeling conscious of it'. In response to taunts from another Labor opponent, Menzies retorted that 'if the honourable member is concerned with my capacity for weeping, I can tell him that I have restrained it manfully ever since he came here'. Of H V (Bert) Evatt, the Leader of the Opposition from 1951-1960, Menzies remarked that 'just as I may be remembered as 'Pig-iron Bob', so my distinguished opponent should go down in history as 'Bandwagon Bert'.

Menzies exhibited some of his most memorable humour at public rallies when responding to hecklers from his audiences. While many of his parliamentary colleagues would simply let these hurls 'go straight to the keeper', Menzies chose to play these with his bat. His 'comebacks' to these interjections were typically quick off the mark and cheeky, drawing laughter and applause from the audience. When confronted by a heckler who cried that 'I would not vote for you if you were the Archangel Gabriel', Menzies replied, 'If I were the Archangel Gabriel, madam, I'm afraid you would not be in my constituency'. To another heckler who asked, 'Wotcha gonna do about 'ousing', Menzies' reply was 'Put an 'h' in front of it'. In response to a persistent heckler at Brighton Town Hall in Victoria, Menzies said, 'I have no objection to your speaking in this hall provided you either do so some other night or that you pay half the cost of the hiring of it tonight'. Earning a public reputation for his rapid riposte at such events, Menzies once remarked that he could swing on to an interjector much faster than a camera.

"We would rather finish this war broke than broken"

Robert Menzies, defending his Government's financial and military programme early in World War II

"Nobody understands this lad better than I do. I was poor at geometry myself – though in politics I've had to get to know quite a deal about angles"

Robert Menzies, Responding to a Moss Vale schoolboy petitioning the Prime Minister to have geometry cut out of the syllabus

"My colleague Jack McEwen has been nicknamed 'Black Jack'. Now and again I address him as 'Black', and occasionally, when in highbrow mode, I call him 'Le Noir'. That's only when I don't want other Country Party men to know what I'm talking about"

Robert Menzies, referring to Deputy Prime Minister and Country Party Leader, John (Jack) McEwen, who earned the moniker 'Black Jack' for his dark 'beetle-browed' appearance and temper when crossed.

"I chanced on a director of The Times, Campbell Stuart, who told me coldly: 'Menzies, you're going to be somewhat uncomfortable here – this is a most intellectual gathering'. Sir, I am going to take the risk of addressing you all as if you were not only intellectual, but intelligent"

Robert Menzies, Royal Institute of International Affairs dinner, 1938

"I hope there'll be no robberies from this pavilion, because I know from my legal knowledge that the first question the police will ask is: 'Who had the Key?'"

Robert Menzies, Opening of Kew Harriers' new club-rooms, 1940

"One thing about bureaucrats is that they never swallow their young. Leave them alone and you'll find them increasing every year"

Robert Menzies, Liberal Rally, Melbourne, 1946

"Don't watch these people, that is what they're paid to do. They are paid to interrupt meetings. They have photographs of themselves being thrown out and they are sent back to Moscow and they get Marx, M.A.R.X. for being photographed in that way"

Robert Menzies, Speech at Public Meeting, Brisbane Town Hall, 15 July 1952

"People generalise, don't they, about people. They can offer you general observations on the Irish, which the Irish enjoy so much that they invent most of them themselves. They offer general observations on the Scots, which the Scots very properly regard as not a useless form of advertising. They even offer general observations about me, and Arthur Calwell, but we survive in spite of it"

Robert Menzies, Opening Speech at Mount Scopus College, Burwood Victoria, 13 September 1960

Interjector: *"Now go on Bob, tell us about inflation and round it off. We've heard you"*

Menzies: *"I wish you would have stood up, because at a glance, in the distance, I wouldn't think I needed to tell you anything about inflation at all"*

Robert Menzies, Speech at Bentleigh, Victoria, 1 December 1960

"When I arrived here this afternoon out at Williamtown, I met the Lord Mayor, Alderman Purdue, which, as you know is a corruption of "par Dieu" - really it is only that the name has been changed that gets him rid of a few rather blasphemous observations in the street"

Robert Menzies, 75th Anniversary Dinner of Chamber of Commerce, Newcastle, 11 September 1961

"I shall never forget this Hall – it has one of the highest platforms in

Australia. It has a great moral for a politician to speak from a very high platform because he is constantly reminded how fast and how far he can fall!"

Robert Menzies, Civic Welcome at Narrabri Town Hall, 29 September 1961

"I saw a Rugby League match on Saturday; I read the rules the night before, not being familiar with this strange game, and when I arrived at the Sydney Cricket Ground, I said to my hosts, "Well, I read the rules last night. There are some points in them I don't fully understand", and they at once offered to make me a referee"

Robert Menzies, Commonwealth Banking Corporation Golden Jubilee Dinner, 16 July 1962

"I had to go and read the Lesson at the Presbyterian Kirk, and the Lesson included the Ten Commandments. No document could be more disturbing to a practicing politician than the Ten Commandments; unless, Your Grace, it is the Sermon on the Mount"

Robert Menzies, Commonwealth Banking Corporation Golden Jubilee Dinner, 16 July 1962

"When people in England jest to me about the lowly origins of our now thriving and law-abiding Commonwealth, I make the good-natured retort that, though many thousands of convicted persons were sent to America and many thousands to Australia, the records show that the great majority of persons convicted in England during the transportation era remained in England!

Robert Menzies, Jefferson Oration, Charlotteville, Virginia, 4 July 1963

"Of course, you will not overlook the fact that while the thistle now has some association with me or I have with the thistle, the shilling also has an association with me because it's a bob."

Robert Menzies, The Armidale School Speech Day, 11 December 1963

"I rather think that the President made a slight understatement when he said that without the women this organisation could not exist, because the simple truth, of course, is that without women, none of us would be here"

Robert Menzies, Opening of the Sir Leslie Morshead War Veteran Homes, Canberra, 26 April 1964

"I was in bed ill, I was in a weakened condition, I had a couple of doctors looming at me over the foot of the bed and discussing whether I ought to be allowed to go abroad. If they had left that to the electors it might have been a different result"

Robert Menzies, Father of the Year – 1964: Presentation at Hotel Australia, Sydney, 14 August 1964

"When I get back home and the vicar invites me to a concert, I'll expect him to announce: And now Miss Flora Smith will sing for us Hume, Sweet, Hume"

Robert Menzies, joking about English, Scottish and Australian pronunciations after Sir Alec Douglas-Home called him 'Ming-ees' at an Australian Club dinner, 1965

"I had a correspondence - Epistles to the Bishops - and one advantage I had over the Apostle Paul was that when he wrote an Epistle to the Romans or to the Corinthians or whatever it might be, as far as I know there was no reply. But I had replies"

Robert Menzies, Young Liberal Rally, Hawthorn Town Hall, Melbourne Victoria, 21 May 1965

"May I tell you that I'm here and my wife is here because we both suffer from an enormous admiration and a deep affection for Sir Charles Bickerton Blackburn, now to be known, as I realise, as Chancellor Emeritus. Might I suggest, Sir, that you should do something about Prime Ministers"

Robert Menzies, Dinner in Honour of Sir Charles Bickerton Blackburn, Chancellor Emeritus, University of Sydney, Sydney, 12 November 1965

24

Others on Menzies

As one of the pre-eminent public figures that loomed large over Australia and indeed the Commonwealth for a number of decades, Menzies naturally attracted a myriad of summations, appraisals and tributes from media commentators, academics, political friends and foes, fellow statesmen and world leaders. Most of these observations touched on his personal qualities, his professional success as a speaker, legal advocate and parliamentarian; and his achievements as a prime minister and statesman. Taken collectively, they serve to paint a portrait of a man who was at once a traditionalist and an innovator, an idealist and a realist, an adversary and a friend, a public statesman and a private family man. While noteworthy reflections of Menzies were offered at various occasions throughout his career, it was his retirement as Prime Minister in January 1966 and death in May 1978 that elicited the greatest outflow of public reflections on a man who had acquitted his wealth of talent and experience in high office to chart the course of modern Australia. At each juncture, his accomplishments and flaws were acknowledged by supporters and opponents alike. Even long after his death, his legacy and achievements have continued to be cited by contemporary leaders from both sides of the political divide.

As expected, Menzies' retirement as Prime Minister on January 20, 1966, evoked a flurry of media commentary from around the country. Despite some critical observations, the press coverage of Menzies' departure was largely positive, doing much to shed light on the substantial legacy he left as Prime Minister. Newspaper editorials frequently alluded to both his vision and enterprise in founding the Liberal Party and his 'staying power' as Australia's longest serving Prime Minister. Lauding Menzies as a 'great parliamentarian', *The Age* editorialised that Menzies had become an 'institution' at home and abroad with 'almost a generation of voters' knowing no other national leader. The paper remarked how 'the brilliant and sharp-tongued young barrister has mellowed into the father-figure, the emblem of stability and sound sense'.[31]

Referring to the 'snowy-haired patriarch of the British Commonwealth', *The Australian* appeared to concur with Menzies' own assessment that 'education is probably the area where he made his greatest contribution'.[32] While praising his electoral success and ability as a parliamentarian, *The Australian* sounded a more critical note on some aspects of his legacy. According to the national broadsheet, Australia's economic growth under Menzies was comparatively modest and his government's foreign policy was too subservient to the agenda of the United States.[33] The paper's editorial concluded with the rather cool assessment that 'while Sir Robert presided over us so well and achieved so much personally, it can't be said that Australia has emerged as a notable pace-setter in any field of human activity'.[34]

The *Sydney Morning Herald* was similarly qualified, editorialising that 'the Menzies era was in many ways a splendid era – dignified, prosperous and sedate. But it was not an era of political or intellectual excitement.'[35] The Sydney broadsheet concluded that while 'Sir Robert Menzies was a great Prime Minister', it declared 'it is time for a change'.[36] The Australian press generally appreciated the statesmanship of Menzies and his accomplishments in office but welcomed the prospect of change in the political tailwinds that Harold Holt appeared to offer. However, as former Prime Minister John Howard convincingly documented in *The Menzies Era*, the seeds of reform in such areas as education, health care, foreign policy, defence, trade and the economy had already been sown and cultivated by Menzies himself, a legacy that appeared to have escaped the attention of some in the press.

The international response to Menzies' retirement on 20 January was swift with generous tributes from both Australia's traditional allies and Asia Pacific neighbours. Declaring Menzies as 'cast in the same mould as Sir Winston Churchill', the British Prime Minister, Harold Wilson, said 'Sir Robert is a great character and a great world figure, symbolic of all that is best in the Commonwealth concept'.[37] The *London Times* commented that 'he has dominated the Australian scene since 1949, but he moulded the Liberal Party and helped to make his country's policy long before the electoral victory that year'.[38] Across the Atlantic, US President Lyndon Johnson said that even after his departure from the public stage, 'the United States would always listen to what Sir Robert had to say because he would still be speaking with the authority of a statesman for Freedom'. President Johnson noted that throughout his prime ministership, Menzies had been 'a friend of the American people' and 'the trusted colleague of four American Presidents'. The *Washington Post* called Sir Robert 'probably the most completely successful public man of his time'.[39] In New Zealand, the Prime Minister Keith Holyoake said 'Sir Robert's decision to retire from political life marked an end to the Parliamentary career of Australia's most outstanding, successful and colourful leader'.[40]

As a reflection of Australia's deeper ties to its own region, cultivated under the Menzies years, the tributes from Asia Pacific leaders were warm. From Kuala Lumpur, the former Malaysian Prime Minister Tunku Abdul Rahman said that Sir Robert's retirement was 'a great loss to Australia which he has served so well and so honourably'. He added that 'He will be greatly missed at Commonwealth conferences, where he has always been a great friend of Malaysia'.[41] In Singapore, the Prime Minister, Lee Kuan Yew, remarked that 'for anyone to stay in office continuously for 16 or 17 years, when elections have to be held every three years is quite an achievement'. The Singaporean leader noted that 'this is not a phenomenon to be explained away easily – other than the fact that Sir Robert Menzies has represented what the majority of Australians would like to see in Australia – prosperity, expansion and a good image abroad'.[42] From

Colombo, the Prime Minister of (then) Ceylon, Dudley Senanayake, said he was personally sorry to hear of Menzies' retirement, remarking that 'Sir Robert has had a personal affection for our country and our people'. As a mark of Menzies' longevity at the helm of Australia, Senanayake noted that 'Australia and Sir Robert have become synonymous'. In Australia, meanwhile, the new Prime Minister, Harold Holt, moved a motion to honour Menzies' long service to parliament and the nation as soon as Federal Parliament resumed in March 1966. With speeches from Sir Robert's old deputy, John McEwen, the ALP leader, Arthur Calwell, and Holt himself, the tributes were once again generous in both their general tone and assessment of Sir Robert's legacy.

With the death of Menzies in May 1978, the nation and indeed the world again paused to remember his illustrious accomplishments. The then Prime Minister, Malcolm Fraser, told parliament that Australians would have 'memories of him as a Prime Minister who strove to enrich the resources, the opportunities and the talent of this nation...'[43] Lauding Menzies as 'one of the most effective politicians in Australia's history', The ALP member for Lalor and 'godfather' to the Labor left, Dr Jim Cairns, recalled that Menzies 'had a way of identifying the attitudes of the average Australian and appealing very vividly, clearly, and incisively to those attitudes'.[44] Remembering Menzies' legacy from abroad, the US President Jimmy Carter referred to Sir Robert as 'a great statesman whose leadership and influence extended far beyond Australia'.[45] The Prime Minister of Britain, James Callaghan, spoke of 'his courage, his devotion to duty and his wisdom (which) have ensured him an honoured place in the history of our time'.[46] Appreciating the enduring implications of the Menzies legacy for our Asia Pacific region, Singapore's Prime Minister, Lee Kuan Yew, paid tribute to both Menzies' personal qualities and the contribution he made as Prime Minister to Australia and the Asia Pacific region.

More recently, the homages paid to his legacy have been no less forthcoming with Prime Minister John Howard in 1996 making the case that the key to Menzies' success and longevity as Prime Minister was his ability to appreciate the values, interests and aspirations of the Australian people. Far from representing an opportunistic populist or a pragmatic transactional manager, Howard argued that Menzies was a genuine conviction politician whose agenda and policy programme drew sustenance from a robust and sustained liberal philosophy of individual freedom and personal responsibility. Liberal stalwart, Sir John Carrick, observed in 2000 that the Menzies era was replete with reforms to social security, health care, housing, education, industry, defence, foreign policy and immigration. As testimony to Australia's social and economic progress under Menzies, Carrick cited the dissipation of class structures, the abandonment of the old religious sectarianism and a palpable rise in national living standards.[47] In August 2014, the most recent successor to Sir Robert in his seat of Kooyong, Josh Frydenberg, observed that 'Menzies' civility, his values and his deep sense of conviction offer a roadmap for any modern day politician' desiring to replicate his legacy.[48]

"When it comes to Parliament I truly consider that Menzies is not only the best debater I have heard, but in my judgment the greatest who ever lived. And I have read Burke, Cicero, Randolph, Churchill, Pitt and Fox"

William Morris ('Billy') Hughes (1862-1952), Australian Prime Minister 1915-1923

"Mr Menzies had 'presence', which gave him dignity without effort. He had a deep dramatic instinct, which taught him to seize the right moments for speaking in the House, the technique of dealing with interjectors, the rapier-like retort, cutting and sometimes cruel, the self-possession and self-awareness of the born actor"

Alfred (Lord) Denning, Lord Justice of Appeal, 1947-48

"He had a beautifully modulated voice, full of power, music and charm. It may have lacked the passionate overtones of the truly great orator, but it was a perfect instrument for the mind behind it. Irony, wit, all the pastel shades of meaning, a genius for the

right word, a fine constancy in holding the thread of an intricate line of argument, were all at his immediate command"
Alfred (Lord) Denning, Lord Justice of Appeal, 1947-48

"I am privileged to call him my friend — a great man, a great Prime Minister, a great figure, perhaps the greatest figure in our Commonwealth today...Under the guidance of Mr. Menzies, the stature of Australia in the world and her influence in world Councils have increased beyond all recognition"
Harold McMillan, Prime Minister of Britain, Speech in Honour of the Rt Hon R G Menzies, Australia Club, London, 22 June 1959

"He is one of the outstanding stalwarts of the free world, a great leader of 10 million people, he stands in the forefront of the few statesmen of the world on whose wisdom, character and courage the hope of free men rests"
Thomas E Dewey, Governor of New York, 6 June 1960

"Sir Robert is a great character and a great world figure, symbolic of all that is best in the Commonwealth concept"
Harold Wilson, Prime Minister of Britain, 21 January 1966

"Here is a man for whom the word 'upright' is so singularly appropriate that we found it running through the whole history of his administration. At no point of time can I recall an instance in which a member of his own Administration or, for that matter, a member of the Public Service, has come under public challenge for some impropriety. He, himself, insisted on the highest standards of integrity and rectitude, and he stands as a model for any Member of Parliament or of an Australian Cabinet"
Harold Holt, Prime Minister of Australia, House of Representatives, 9 March 1966

"I have always thought of Sir Robert Menzies most...for his record of service to the parliamentary institution. He sensed at all times that this institution must be guarded, that it must not be injured in the opinions of the people and that its dignity must be maintained. In that respect, he walked in the footsteps of the

great parliamentarians in the tradition that we have inherited"

Arthur Calwell, ALP Leader of the Opposition, House of Representatives, 9 March 1966

"In personal terms, the period of leadership of Sir Robert Menzies was really phenomenal. He was completely preeminent on the political stage at home and he achieved, as few Australians have done or, maybe, will do, a stature of eminence as an international statesman - an elder statesman who was so regarded throughout the world, for he was widely regarded as an elder statesman not only in his own country and within the Commonwealth of Nations but beyond the bounds of that Commonwealth"

John McEwen, Deputy Prime Minister, House of Representatives, 9 March 1966

"Under the Prime Ministership of Sir Robert Menzies, Australia was developed as a nation, balancing its devotion to the production of material wealth against its desire for educational and cultural advancement. One of the greatest things is that as it developed and grew richer it provided equal opportunity for every citizen"

John McEwen, Deputy Prime Minister, House of Representatives, 9 March 1966

"I have always respected his great ability; I have always respected his great integrity. I've admired his single-minded devotion to the cause he served. His importance to the Liberal Party cannot be overestimated. He founded the Liberal Party, he wrote its platform, he moulded its attitudes and philosophy, he was the Liberal Party"

Arthur Calwell, Leader of the Opposition, 1966

"Sir Robert has earned in his own lifetime the respect and admiration of Australians, regardless of their political beliefs"

Lyndon B Johnson, President of the United States (1963-1969), 21 January 1966

"Australia and Sir Robert have become synonymous... Sir Robert's retirement from the political field will be a loss to the Commonwealth, of which he is the reigning undisputed elder

statesman"

Dudley Senanayake, Prime Minister of Ceylon, 21 January 1966

"I venture to predict that when in future centuries people come to write the history of Australia in the 20ᵗʰ century and they come to look at the influences that have made Australia what it was in the middle of the 20ᵗʰ century, one of the most distinguished names to be recorded, will be the work of Sir Robert Menzies. He did so much to give national character to what was happening in Australia during a period when we were growing up to an independent and rather assertive nationhood of our own"

Sir Paul Hasluck, Governor-General of Australia (1969-1974), 21 March 1973

"He was one of the great men of his era. He had a commanding presence, a powerful intellect and a rare eloquence. His robust approach to life enabled him to make more than Australia's contribution to the world's quest for peace and stability in an age of rapid and revolutionary changes. He has left his imprint on the history of Australia and of the region"

Lee Kuan Yew, Prime Minister of Singapore (1959-1990), 19 May 1978

"He was an immensely distinguished Australian whose contribution to his country and to the development of the Commonwealth will long be remembered"

Queen Elizabeth II, 16 May 1978

"His courage, his devotion to duty and his wisdom have earned him an honoured place in the history of our times"

James Callaghan, Prime Minister of Britain, 16 May 1978

"He had a fierce burning faith in freedom and democracy and a warm and deep understanding of human nature. He married these two things together in shaping his vision for the future"

Margaret Thatcher, British Conservative Party Leader, 16 May 1978

"Sir Robert was a great political leader who not only enjoyed tremendous respect from the Australian people but he served to make Australia known and respected worldwide. Australia will long enjoy the benefits, that he, during his period of leadership brought to this country"

Sir John McEwen, former Deputy Prime Minister of Australia, 16 May 1978

"He led Australia in the most prosperous period of its history. His contribution to Australian life can be seen in two of his greatest policies. He combined individualistic liberalism with a commitment to social welfare; and while committed to the British connection he developed the American alliance"

Peter Coleman, former NSW Liberal leader, 16 May 1978

"Sir Robert Menzies was a towering Australian political figure, excelling Hughes in intellect, Deakin in staying power, and both Curtin and Chifley in realism. He was also the first Australian statesman with a truly international reputation"

Sir Robert Southey, former Federal president of the Liberal Party, 16 May 1978

"Menzies was without any doubt the finest orator that the Parliament has seen in the past 50 years at least. I think of him as a magnificent orator. And he always maintained a dignity unmatched by many men"

Clyde Cameron, former Labor Minister, 16 May 1978

"Sir Robert was one of the finest men I met and knew and I respected him, as [a] friend even though we were from different parties"

Former Australian Prime Minister, Frank Forde, 16 May 1978

"Sir Robert was one of the most significant and successful political leaders of recent Australian history. A master parliamentary and political tactician, he created the Liberal Party from the fragmented conservative forces of the mid 1940s and welded together a cohesive coalition – which he dominated during a record term as Prime Minister of this country for 17 years"

Bill Hayden, federal Labor Leader of the Opposition, 16 May 1978

"History will record in proper perspective the role he played in establishing Australia in the eyes of the post-war world as an international force to be reckoned with on all fronts"

Sir Charles Court, Premier of Western Australia, 16 March 1978

"Australia has lost one of its best known sons, a man who led a nation for almost two generations. It is a great loss in the nation"

Neville Wran, Premier of New South Wales, 16 March 1978

"The one thing I would say, with very deep conviction, is that he [Sir Robert] did have a concept of Australia as a nation instead of just being six States. In this sense, that he did help to develop a sense of national identity, he did perform a very great service"

Bob Hawke, President of the ACTU & ALP, 16 March 1978

"Sir Robert Menzies has left an indelible mark upon countless facets of Australian life. He will be remembered as a leader, a statesman, a scholar, an ally, a friend, and to his family as a loving and devoted husband, brother and father. He gave to each of these roles the full measure of his being. To this one man, Robert Gordon Menzes, Australia owes an immense debt. It is a debt which future generations of Australians can honour by holding fast to the virtues he brought from his forbears and carried into his life – the virtues of sincerity, integrity, loyalty, steadfastness and courage."

Malcolm Fraser, Australian Prime Minister (1975-1983), 23 May 1978

"During the long period that he was Prime Minister of Australia, Sir Robert Menzies consistently achieved that often elusive balance between the practical and the idealistic which is so necessary to both govern effectively and provide strong political leadership"

John Howard, Sir Robert Menzies Lecture, Melbourne, 18 June 1980

"Sir Robert Menzies was a great statesman. I shall always remember him with affection and gratitude as the most unaffected of men who offered valuable advice without patronising and with a wit

and a simplicity which distilled pure wisdom from a lifetime's experience".

Margaret Thatcher, British Prime Minister (1979-1990), 6 October 1981

"If I were to rate one post-war leader... it would not be one of the legendary European or American figures. It would be Robert Menzies...had Menzies been born in Britain, he would have been that country's prime minister. Had this been the case, Menzies would have ranked with Gladstone and Disraeli"

Richard Nixon, US President (1969-1974), 1982

"Menzies was a true liberal. But he was also a true conservative. He believed deeply in the society into which he was born... Menzies was the kind of intelligent conservative who welcomes social evolution, but tries to guide it in accordance with the best liberal principles"

John Hewson, Sir Robert Menzies Lecture, Melbourne, 29 November 1990

"He [Menzies] enjoyed unprecedented electoral success, partly because he was somebody. People knew what he believed in, and roughly where his priorities lay. He enjoyed an unparalleled term of federal success for an additional reason: he somehow managed to find a balance between two important roles. Firstly he handed out to the electorate such concessions, gifts and challenges as the nation could normally afford. Secondly he so governed that in the normal year the nation's wealth steadily increased"

Professor Geoffrey Blainey, Sir Robert Menzies Lecture, Melbourne, 1991

"The fact is that the Menzies era provided good government of integrity, high achievement and strong leadership which Australians returned to office again and again because it was attuned to the aspirations of the great mainstream of Australian society, because it delivered on what it promised — and, it is true, because of the internal divisions within the ranks of its political opponents"

John Howard, Sir Robert Menzies Lecture, Melbourne, 18 November 1996

"Menzies' intense Australianness was highlighted in the political relationship he had with the Australian people. He articulated the hopes and concerns of the Australians of his time more effectively, more representatively and for a longer period than any other national leader"

John Howard, Sir Robert Menzies Lecture, Melbourne, 18 November 1996

"Menzies' political genius lay in that basic affinity with the aspirations of the Australian people. He understood the priority they placed on jobs, on rising living standards, on home ownership, on high economic growth, on a sense of national unity, and on opportunities for their children that were greater than they themselves had experienced. And he developed priorities in national policymaking and a role for national government that enabled those aspirations to be achieved"

John Howard, Sir Robert Menzies Lecture, Melbourne, 18 November 1996

"Menzies had his finger on the pulse of the Australian nation in a way that few other leaders have matched and none have surpassed. But the quality of his political leadership did not lie in perceiving or anticipating every shift in public opinion. He responded to public opinion, but he also shaped it. He respected it, but he also guided it. He knew the difference between short-term public opinion and long-term public interest"

John Howard, Sir Robert Menzies Lecture, Melbourne, 18 November 1996

"Menzies valued a broad-based political philosophy because he knew that it was from such a philosophy that Liberalism derived its enduring values — values such as individual freedom, choice, diversity, opportunity, and the importance of strong families and communities as bulwarks against the intrusive power of the State"

John Howard, Sir Robert Menzies Lecture, Melbourne, 18 November 1996

"When Menzies had it [the Liberal Party], it was a classic, great, governing party, the broad-based Tory-Party with a strong

appeal to the working class. It had big-minded people, who had been coming through the ranks to be officers in World War II, who saw the good possibilities of government. That's why a bloke like Menzies could create Canberra, why Menzies could focus on universities. He was sort of a classic British Conservative"

Kim Beazley, 1996, quoted by Peter Fitzsimons, *Beazley: A Biography* by Peter Fitzsimons (Sydney: HarperCollins Publishers, 1998), p 418.

"We are now familiar with the extraordinary achievements and the honours bestowed on Sir Robert in his later life. But another part of the Menzies story is how he came from a small country town, on a scholarship, to the city of Melbourne, and with diligence, intellect, and education rose to the leadership of the nation"

Peter Costello, Sir Robert Menzies Lecture, Melbourne, 12 November 1997

"This is Menzies' unpardonable fault: that he sounded as passionate about Britain as about Australia. This is not because Menzies was confused about who he was. Rather, it was to promote those values - freedom under the law, parliamentary institutions and pluralist democracy - which were Britain's gift to Australia and the wider world and to advance Australia as the significant other in what Churchill called the unwritten alliance between Britain and America"

Tony Abbott, Sir Robert Menzies Lecture: the Brother Countries, Melbourne, 17 May 2004

"Sir Robert Menzies, demonstrated he understood the power of education as a force for good, a force for equity and a force for change"

Julia Gillard, Sir Robert Menzies Oration, University of Melbourne, 6 November 2008

"He [Menzies] argued powerfully for a new post-war world based on free enterprise, not central planning; on self-reliance, not a nanny state."

"...the one golden thread which shines as bright today as it did in

Menzies' time is that of freedom."

Malcolm Turnbull, Sir Robert Menzies Memorial Lecture, 8 October 2009.

"Menzies' greatest legacy as a statesman was to lay the foundations of modern Australia. The economic prosperity of the 1950s ensured a good life for larger numbers of Australians than ever before. The Australia, New Zealand, United States Security (ANZUS) Treaty arrived as the bedrock of our security, and the 1957 Commerce Agreement opened up the huge potential of the Japanese market, just as the British market was diminishing. Menzies maintained and broadened the immigration programme commenced by the post World War II Labor Government"

John Howard, Australian Prime Minister (1996-2007), 2014

"In the history of nations there are always giants. They are the handful of men and women who through their courage, their perseverance, their intellect, passion and will, they change the course of their nation. In the life of Australia, Sir Robert Gordon Menzies certainly fits that bill. He is one of our greatest, if not our greatest giant when it comes to the history of modern Australia."

Scott Morrison, Sir Robert Menzies Lecture 2019, Melbourne, 12 March 2019

"Menzies...reached out and built a Party based on enduring truths; the truths of liberalism and liberal democracy that outlive any one individual or the fashion of any one time, truths that unite a rich breadth of thought across our community."

Scott Morrison, Sir Robert Menzies Lecture 2019, Melbourne, 12 March 2019

Endnotes

1 Paul Hasluck, Sir Robert Menzies (The 1979 Daniel Mannix Memorial Lecture) (Carlton: Melbourne University Press, 1980), p 25.
2 David Kemp, *Robert Menzies: The Forgotten People and other Studies in Democracy* (Melbourne: Liberal Party of Australia, 2011), p 14.
3 Kemp, *Robert Menzies*, p 14.
4 Kemp, *Robert Menzies*, p 11.
5 Kemp, *Robert Menzies*, p 12.
6 Kemp, *Robert Menzies*, p 18.
7 Gerard Henderson, "Why Menzies Still Matters", *Quadrant* (online), December 7, 2008, p 19 of 20.
8 Robert Menzies, *The Liberal Creed*, Canberra, 6 April 1964.
9 Kemp, *Robert Menzies*, p 20.
10 John Roskam, 'Liberalism and Social Welfare', in J. R. Nethercote (ed) *Liberalism and the Australian Federation* (Sydney: Federation Press, 2001), p 268
11 Mikayla Novak, 'The Condition of the People', in J. R. Nethercote (ed), Menzies: The Shaping of Modern Australia (Redland Bay [QLD]: Connor Court, 2016), p 202.
12 Leslie Bury, 'Home Savings Grant Bill 1964', Second Reading Speech, House of Representatives, *Hansard,* 5 May, 1994.
13 Novak, 'The Condition of the People', p 203.
14 Novak, 'The Condition of the People', p 201.
15 John Murphy, 'Social Policy and the Family', in Scott Prasser, J. R. Nethercote and John Warhurst, *The Menzies Era: A Reappraisal of Government, Politics and Policy* (Sydney: Hale and Iremonger, 1995) p 235.
16 J J Pincus, "Federation in the Menzies Years' in Nethercote, *Menzies*, p 312.
17 Peter Coleman, quoted in *The Australian*, Tuesday, 14 May 1978.
18 John Roskam, 'Liberalism and Social Welfare', London, 6 July 1964, p 270.
19 Robert Menzies, First Baillieu Lecture, pp 9-10.
20 John Murphy, *Imagining the Fifties: Private Sentiment and Political Culture in Menzies Australia* (Sydney: UNSW Press, 2000), p 83.
21 Henry Ergas and J J Pincus, 'The Wealth of the Nation', Neathercote, *Menzies*, p 133.
22 Novak, 'The Condition of the People', p 212.
23 Novak, 'The Condition of the People', p 213.
24 Graeme Starr, 'Menzies and Post-War Prosperity' in Nethercote, *Liberalism*, pp 190-191.
25 Starr, 'Menzies and Post-War Prosperity', p 191.
26 Roskam, 'Liberalism and Social Welfare', p 273.

27 Menzies, 'First Baillieu Lecture', p 3.

28 Robert Menzies, Opening Speech, Canberra Conference, 13 October 1944

29 Anne Henderson, 'Robert Menzies - War and Peace', in Nethercote, *Menzies*, p 38.

30 Margaret Fitzherbert, *So Many Firsts: Liberal Women from Enid Lyons to the Turnbull Era* (Sydney: Federation Press, 2009), p 43.

31 "A Leader Leaves the Scene", *The Age*, Friday, January 21, 1966, p 5.

32 "Evaluating the Reign of Menzies", *The Australian*, Friday, January 21, 1966, p 4.

33 "Evaluating the Reign of Menzies", *Australian*, p 4.

34 "Evaluating the Reign of Menzies", *Australian*, p 4.

35 "All Change: The Menzies Era", *Sydney Morning Herald*, Friday, January 21, 1966, p 2.

36 "All Change", *Herald*, p 2.

37 Harold Wilson quoted by *The Age*, Friday, January 21, 1966, p 7.

38 The London Times quoted by *The Age*, Friday, January 21, 1966, p 7.

39 The Washington Post quoted by *The Age*, Friday, January 21, 1966, p 7.

40 Keith Holyoake quoted by T*he Age*, Friday, January 21, 1966, p 7.

41 Tunku Abdul Rahman quoted by *The Age*, Friday, January 21, 1966, p 7.

42 Lee Kuan Yew quoted by *The Age*, Friday, January 21, 1966, p 7.

43 Malcolm Fraser, 'Death of the Right Honourable Sir Robert Gordon Menzies Speech', Hansard, Cth. Parliamentary Debates, House of Representatives, 23 May 1978.

44 Jim Cairns quoted by Bill Hayden, 'Death of the Right Honourable Sir Robert Gordon Menzies Speech', Hansard, Cth. Parliamentary Debates, House of Representatives, 23 May 1978.

45 Jimmy Carter quoted by Malcolm Fraser, 'Death of the Right Honourable Sir Robert Gordon Menzies Speech', Hansard, Cth. Parliamentary Debates, House of Representatives, 23 May 1978.

46 James Callaghan quoted by Malcolm Fraser, 'Death of the Right Honourable Sir Robert Gordon Menzies Speech', Hansard, Cth. Parliamentary Debates, House of Representatives, 23 May 1978.

47 Sir John Carrick, Liberal Heritage – An Australian Perspective, 2000, pp 16-17, cited in Graeme Starr, "Menzies and Prosperity", in John Nethercote (ed), *Liberalism and the Australian Federation* (Sydney: The Federation Press, 2001), pp 194-195.

48 Josh Frydenberg MP, "2014 Sir Robert Menzies Lecture: Menzies' Roadmap for Asia Still Guides Us Today", 14 August 2014, Parliament House, Victoria.

Index

www.ingramcontent.com/pod-product-compliance
Lightning Source LLC
Chambersburg PA
CBHW071854270326
41929CB00013B/2222